THE CBT WORKBOOK FOR MENTAL HEALTH

Evidence-Based Exercises to
TRANSFORM NEGATIVE THOUGHTS
and MANAGE YOUR WELL-BEING

SIMON A. REGO, PsyD, AND SARAH FADER

FOREWORD BY JONATHAN E. ALPERT, MD, PhD

ROCKRIDGE
PRESS

To my parents, Barbara and Tony Rego, for the unwavering support you provided me on my long path to becoming a cognitive behavioral psychologist. To my patients, particularly in the Bronx, New York, for inspiring me every day with your resilience and determination. And to my beautiful wife, Adriana, and two beautiful boys, Diego and Sebastian, for reminding me each day of what's important in life. —SAR

To my parents, Elizabeth and Jeffrey Fader, and my beautiful children, Ari and Samara. And to all those who want to change the way they think to better their lives. —SF

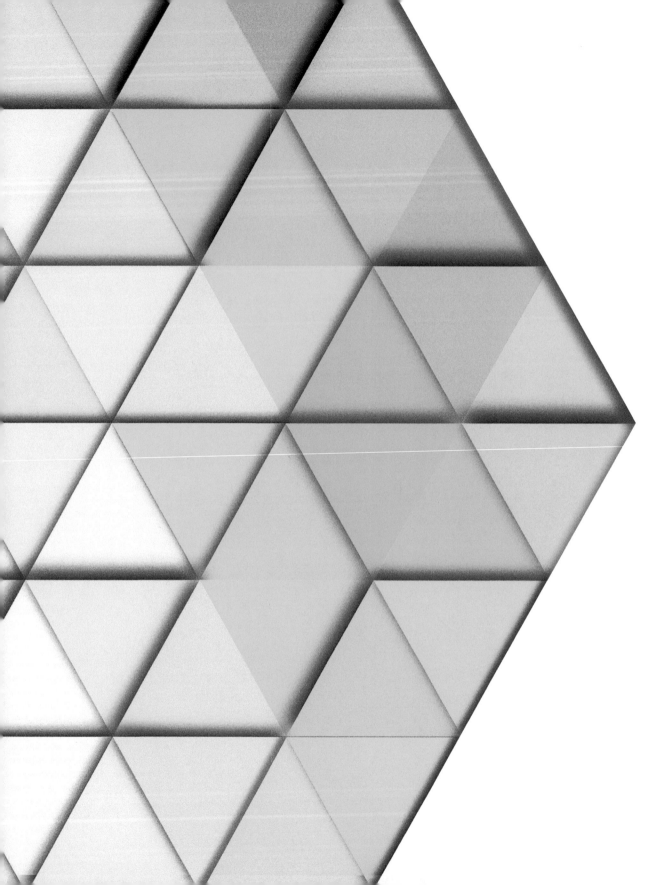

Contents

Foreword

who are open to the possibility of personal growth and change. Award-winning psychologist Simon Rego, PsyD, a consummate clinician and educator beloved by colleagues and students, and Sarah Fader, known widely for her mental health advocacy and eloquent writing, have teamed up to provide a lively, warm, practical, and uniquely accessible guide to cognitive behavioral therapy (CBT).

Among the most exciting and impactful innovations in the field of mental health over the past several decades has been the development of short-term forms of psychotherapy that are pragmatic, goal-oriented, and well-studied. Of all these evidenced-based therapies, CBT sits atop the broadest and most impressive evidence base.

The skills and principles of CBT are now applied widely to help treat diagnosable disorders such as social anxiety, depression, posttraumatic stress disorder, obsessive-compulsive disorder, eating disorders, and substance use disorders. But the benefits of CBT extend well beyond the realm of clinical diagnoses. CBT has also proven useful for a wide range of common human problems such as stress, strained relationships, anger, procrastination, and low self-esteem, to name just a few of the important topics this book touches on. Elements of CBT are increasingly incorporated into education and training programs in schools and workplaces because of their documented efficacy and far-reaching value for improving our everyday quality of life. Light on jargon and replete with wisdom and valuable exercises, *The CBT Workbook for Mental Health* promises to become the go-to resource for individuals interested in pursuing CBT on their own or who wish to incorporate this book as homework with a skilled therapist.

As a psychiatrist who has often prescribed reading or "bibliotherapy" to patients (and myself!), it is a joy to discover this remarkable workbook. I expect this book will be read carefully and returned to frequently—even by initially skeptical readers and those

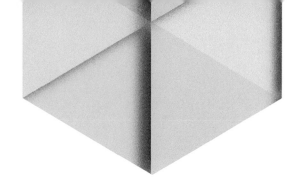

currently burdened by challenges that make routine tasks a chore. The authors clearly understand and empathize with the challenges we all face. Their writing is engaging, encouraging, and nonjudgmental. They neither patronize us nor let us off the hook easily. They furnish a trove of inventive, useful, and feasible exercises, each introduced by a concise statement of principles and objectives and even the estimated time for completion. Much like musicians and athletes, readers who practice these exercises—perhaps tentatively and reluctantly at first—will find their CBT muscles growing steadily stronger. For many readers, what starts off as thoughtful tips and interesting exercises will likely get incorporated as novel frameworks for thinking and behaving and developing positive habits for more healthy lives.

On behalf of all of us who know that life is not always easy, my admiring thanks to the authors who have given us a wealth of actionable insights and steps to support us on our journey.

JONATHAN E. ALPERT, MD, PhD

Dorothy and Marty Silverman University Chair of Psychiatry and Behavioral Sciences

Professor of Psychiatry, Neuroscience, and Pediatrics

Psychiatrist-in-Chief

Montefiore Medical Center

Albert Einstein College of Medicine

Introduction

ALTHOUGH WE ARE NOT ALWAYS AWARE OF THEM, our thoughts impact our feelings about ourselves, the world around us, and our future. They also influence how we behave. Since you're embarking on this workbook, chances are you realize that your thoughts and behaviors are having a negative impact on your life and you're ready to do something about it. Good for you!

Cognitive behavioral therapy (CBT), which this workbook is based on, is a form of talk therapy that has been used with great success since the 1960s to help people feel better about themselves and live more satisfying lives. The basic premise in CBT is that by changing your thoughts and behaviors, you can change the way you feel. This can help increase your self-esteem, clarify what's important to you, and empower you to accomplish your goals. In this workbook, rather than talking it out with a therapist, you'll be writing it out for yourself. You'll also be encouraged to take certain actions, some of which will likely be out of your comfort zone, as change often comes from trying something new. Of course, if you feel you need more help than this book can offer, you can always find a good therapist to talk to.

CBT has been found to be helpful for people with anxiety, depression, addiction, stress disorders such as posttraumatic stress disorder (PTSD), obsessive-compulsive disorder (OCD), and other psychological problems. If you fall into one of these categories, you'll learn techniques that can help. However, you certainly don't have to be diagnosed with a mental health disorder to reap the benefits of CBT. CBT has had excellent results when practiced by people in their everyday lives—from decreased stress levels and improved self-esteem to more assertiveness and motivation. In fact, in some places, CBT is starting to be taught in schools, to give children the basics of emotional health management along with their math, reading, and other skills.

CBT resonates with many people because it teaches practical skills to help us feel better. For example, we might be convinced that we know someone else is thinking something negative about us and, as a result, we feel bad. In CBT, this is a cognitive distortion called *mind reading*. Or maybe we think that the worst thing will happen (e.g., "If I go on an airplane, it will crash") even though there's no proof to that effect. In CBT, these cognitive distortions are called *fortune telling* and *catastrophizing*. In this workbook, you'll have an opportunity to practice skills to increase your awareness of cognitive distortions and choose a different way of thinking. By learning to identify and correct cognitive distortions, you will have a clearer and more balanced way of thinking, which can improve your mood and increase your willingness to do things you might not otherwise be willing to do.

Another reason why CBT resonates with so many people is because it's solution-oriented. The focus is on changing your thought patterns and behaviors in the here and now, in order to help you feel better, solve problems you may be experiencing, and achieve goals that are important to you. In this workbook, you will learn how versatile CBT is and feel for yourself how powerful it can be in helping improve your sense of well-being.

How to Use This Workbook

are designed to help you identify your negative thoughts and problematic behaviors and start transforming them into more adaptive, productive ones. Each chapter discusses a different common struggle—low self-esteem; shaky relationships; stress, anxiety, and anger; guilt and shame; and constant cravings—and offers various techniques and exercises to help you better manage the issue.

The exercises, which take anywhere from 10 to 30 minutes, are meant to be *practiced* regularly in your daily life. Changing your thinking and behavior patterns takes time and practice, so consistency is the key to success. If you devote 30 minutes each day to practicing these CBT exercises, you should start to feel the benefits almost immediately. And the beauty of CBT is that there are no side effects to doing it more. In fact, the more time and effort you put into learning the skills, the bigger the difference they will make in how you feel in the long term. That's the goal: to notice your mood improving and old patterns of thinking and behaving changing! So use these techniques freely and often.

We suggest you initially work through the book chapter by chapter, as some areas may build upon others. You'll find a variety of exercises such as thought records, mindfulness meditation, journaling, increasing physical activity, and role-playing. Some

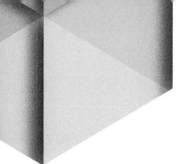

exercises might resonate more with you, but we encourage you to try all the different techniques at least once so you know which ones work the best for you. We feel confident that you *will* find many exercises beneficial. You can then make those exercises your go-to tools for when life inevitably brings challenging events your way. If there's an exercise you particularly like, keep practicing it. If there's one you don't like, don't force yourself to do it. The point of this workbook is to give you tangible tools that can help you, so flip around in the book as much as you want to once you've had a chance to practice all the techniques.

Just remember that changing your negative thought and behavior patterns takes time, so it's important to be patient in the process. We do believe, however, that you will see positive changes take place in the way you think, feel, and act by engaging in these simple, short exercises. So let's delve into how CBT can better your mindset and improve your life, starting with a quick lesson on understanding CBT.

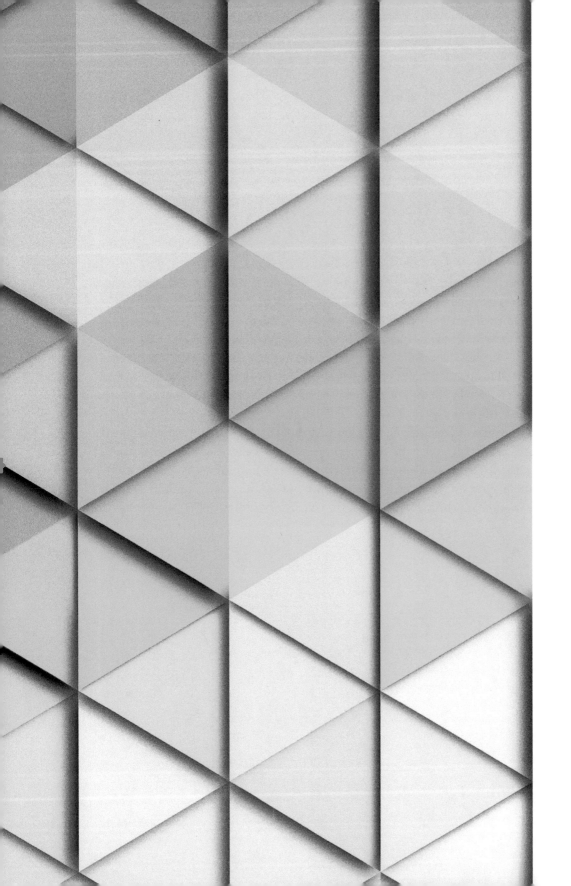

1

UNDERSTANDING COGNITIVE BEHAVIORAL THERAPY (CBT)

The way people think about things and what they choose to do or not do have a substantial influence on their mood, and vice versa. Cognitive behavioral therapy (CBT) is a form of psychotherapy that helps you understand how your thoughts and actions can influence how you feel. CBT originated in the 1960s, when Dr. Aaron Beck, an eminent psychiatrist at the University of Pennsylvania, merged what he termed cognitive therapy with the already established behavior therapy, initially to treat depression. This approach eventually became known as cognitive behavior therapy.

In addition to CBT benefiting anyone dealing with everyday life challenges, since the 1960s CBT has been studied for a number of mental health disorders, including anxiety and depression, with the research suggesting it is highly effective—in fact, often as potent as medications—in bringing relief from symptoms and enhancing quality of life, enjoyment, and satisfaction. For example, research in *Clinical Psychology Review* found that treatment response rates across anxiety disorders averaged 49.5 percent after CBT treatment and 53.6 percent at follow-up. Other studies have found response rates ranging from 50 to 75 percent for social anxiety and 70 to 80 percent for primary insomnia. In many instances, such as the treatment of major depression, panic disorder, and obsessive-compulsive disorder (OCD), CBT can be combined with medications to optimize the benefits, and these effects remain strong and significant up to two years after treatment. To sum up, based on more than 50 years of research, there's no doubt that CBT is a well-established, safe, and effective option for treating many mental health conditions.

Most experts agree that CBT should be the first approach therapists use for people seeking out talk therapy for a problem because there is more evidence that CBT works than any other form of psychotherapy. Unlike some other forms of talk therapy, CBT is short-term and goal-oriented. While there are some exceptions, many people see their CBT therapists for about 12 to 20 visits, once a week for 45 minutes, over the course of about three to five months. In CBT, you work primarily in the here and now and set practical goals aimed at helping you feel better and live a more fulfilling life. In CBT, the emphasis is on learning new skills to change negative thought patterns and problematic behaviors to improve your mood and quality of life.

In some cases, it's useful to have a CBT-trained therapist to guide you through the therapeutic process. In many cases, however, what makes the treatment so successful is the person's *willingness* (i.e., motivation and commitment) to practice the exercises between sessions. Therefore, you can use this workbook as a stand-alone resource or as a "homework" resource if you are in treatment. Either way, perhaps the most potent ingredient in CBT is putting in the time to practice. And once learned, the CBT skills you develop will empower you to feel confident enough to manage future life challenges on your own.

HOW DOES CBT WORK?

As mentioned, CBT relies on practical tools to help you change your thoughts and actions to work through complex emotions. This therapy helps you gain insight into patterns of thinking and behaving you may not have been aware of. At the same time, it

helps you focus on making changes, such as by learning to separate your rational mind from your emotional mind (and then integrate them) while also learning to establish new patterns of behavior. For some people, that doesn't come intuitively. Remember, CBT is a skills-based approach, and like learning any new skill, it can take time to become good at it.

Before we move on, let's debunk two myths about CBT:

1. **CBT is not about thinking positively.** It is about thinking rationally. Sometimes life is not positive. We must radically accept that and then decide what we are going to do, *despite* what's not positive and *because of* what's not positive.

2. **CBT doesn't teach you to ignore your feelings.** CBT is all about your feelings! However, the emphasis is on gaining a clearer understanding of how your feelings influence your thoughts and actions, and vice versa, because the easiest way to impact your feelings is by focusing on your thoughts and actions.

CBT proposes that, too often, we make mistakes in how we think about things such as *emotional reasoning*. Let's say you're nervous because a friend hasn't called or texted you back. You may conclude your friend is angry with you. Even though you don't know what your friend is actually feeling, you react emotionally to the belief that your friend is angry with you. You might then avoid that friend or not return their calls. The problem here is that you never get the opportunity to see if what you thought was actually true, much less correct the situation if your friend really was angry with you for some reason. As a result, you miss a learning opportunity, and the problematic beliefs and behavioral patterns persist.

CBT teaches you how to identify cognitive distortions (see page 7), challenge your beliefs to confirm whether they are accurate, and then change them if they are not. A thought record is often helpful here. If you were working with a CBT therapist, they would have you write down your automatic thoughts (in this example, "My friend is angry at me") and then identify what cognitive distortions may be impacting these ideas and what evidence you have for and against this belief. (You'll have a chance to make a thought record soon; see page 9.)

When the situation is emotionally charged, it can be challenging to tease out what's real and what's distorted. However, if you're able to step back and scrutinize your thoughts, you may realize that you don't know if your friend is angry at you, because you haven't asked. You might realize that you're engaging in "*mind reading*." Without asking, you can't know what someone else is thinking, because you can't read minds. Once you recognize the cognitive distortion, you can now reframe the thought (i.e.,

change it into a more balanced, rational, and realistic thought). Remember, this is not the same as thinking positively. The goal here is to try to think of things as objectively and accurately as possible, and perhaps even test out your thoughts in the real world so that you can confirm or refute them; for example, you can ask your friend if they are angry with you.

What Is Behavioral Activation?

Behavioral activation is a technique originally used in CBT for managing depression. The aim is to increase your participation in activities that bring you a sense of accomplishment or pleasure. Engaging in pleasurable or productive activities can help change the way you think and feel and often can motivate you to do even more activities over time. Engaging in behavioral activation helps you understand how your behaviors influence your emotions and thoughts. Perhaps you feel anxious about an upcoming test and you keep thinking you're going to fail it. You're supposed to meet up with a study group, but you're convinced it won't help. Rather than canceling your appointment and focusing on your negative thoughts or doing something unproductive to distract yourself from them, go through the motions one step at a time: gather your materials, leave the house, get in your car, drive to the location, greet your study group, share your concerns about the test, and study. Each step you take shows you that you're capable of taking action, feels good, and makes the next step more likely to be completed. You can then congratulate yourself for getting to your destination. Although it may have seemed like a difficult or even impossible task, you made it there! And chances are that studying for the test will help you feel better, too.

WHAT CAN CBT BE USED FOR?

Everyone can benefit from CBT. While it's best known for treating issues such as anxiety and depression, CBT has many applications. For example, you may be struggling with intrusive thoughts or compulsive behaviors that are impacting your ability to function daily or in certain situations. If so, using the techniques from CBT can help with these struggles. Some of the uses of CBT might surprise you. It's such a versatile set of techniques that it can improve many different conditions and support you in everyday life. The following is just a small sampling of reasons you might pursue CBT.

Growing Self-Esteem and Self-Acceptance

CBT is a wonderful tool for learning about yourself, your emotional triggers, and which cognitive distortions are common to you. Once you're aware of your negative thought patterns, you can choose which thoughts have meaning and which ones you can disregard. When you are better able to handle intrusive negative thoughts, you can take action on more helpful thoughts and, as a result, gain more confidence in yourself. When you are more confident, your self-esteem increases. In addition, as you make progress toward goals that are meaningful to you, you feel a sense of accomplishment and pleasure in doing so, which also increases your self-esteem. Your emotions will no longer be controlling your actions; rather, you will make conscious choices about how to move forward. Of course, there are some aspects of ourselves and our lives that we cannot change and are not distorted. Fortunately, CBT is also a wonderful tool for helping us learn to accept the less desirable aspects of ourselves and our lives and still feel good despite them.

Strengthening Relationships

CBT is a great tool for learning how to better communicate with important people in your life. You can learn how to not take things personally when you're talking to friends, coworkers, significant others, or even strangers. Communication in any type of relationship can be quite challenging. With CBT, you can be more aware of any cognitive distortions you're having during your exchanges with others. One common distortion that many of us fall into using is *mind reading*. We assume that we know what someone is thinking or feeling without checking with that person. When you learn CBT skills, you will learn to catch, challenge, and change that distortion and find proactive ways to communicate effectively with other people in all types of situations.

Managing Stress, Anxiety, and Anger

Life is full of stressors, some of which make us anxious, angry, or just generally stressed. We all have our unique stressors. CBT offers concrete methods to identify them and manage the issues. For example, you might suffer from anxiety and predict the worst will happen in a given situation. That's called *catastrophizing*, and you can learn how to catch, challenge, and change that distortion with CBT skills. When you learn about cognitive distortions, you will start to recognize them more easily when you're in a

situation that provokes stress, anxiety, or anger. When you are facing these situations, CBT can provide you with tools that will help you get back into a reasonable frame of mind and calm your response, allowing you to select the most productive action available to you.

Letting Go of Guilt and Shame

Guilt is associated with thoughts of regret for things we did or did not do. While nearly everyone feels guilty and has regrets about certain things in life, there's nothing you can do to change the past. The best course of action is to examine how these thoughts and feelings are impacting you in the present, take accountability for your past actions, and let go of the guilty feelings by catching, challenging, and changing thoughts associated with guilt, using your CBT skills. CBT techniques will show you how to acknowledge the thoughts that are causing your guilt and how to reframe them so you're able to see things in a more balanced way and respond as needed. When you feel shame, it's typically because you believe you have violated a social norm. Sometimes we feel shame from within; other times, outside forces attempt to shame us. CBT teaches that excessive shame is often a product of distorted thinking, and even when it isn't, it is often not helpful to dwell on it. Therefore, the more you learn to identify when you feel shame, the better able you will be to start reframing your thoughts and taking productive action in order to help diminish the feelings of shame.

Coping with Constant Cravings

People who struggle with constant cravings—whether for substances such as drugs, alcohol, or food, or impulses for other potentially problematic behaviors like shopping, gambling, or even extreme sports—can benefit from learning CBT tools. CBT can complement treatments for substance abuse issues and associated mental health problems or can be used alone to combat problematic cravings and impulses that have not yet reached clinical levels of severity (at which point CBT is often combined with medications). You will learn how to identify and manage cues and triggers, as well as the emotions, thoughts, and behaviors associated with your cravings, and break them down to see their components. That way, you can better understand how to cope with your cravings and impulses and make different choices.

Managing Psychological Disorders

CBT is a short-term, present-focused, structured approach that allows people dealing with psychological disorders to change the way they feel through modifying their thought processes and behavioral patterns. This sort of structured treatment approach can be an extremely helpful method for teaching how to manage symptoms and live a fuller life. While CBT may help people manage their psychological symptoms, it may take more than a workbook to help them get better. If you're already in therapy, this book shouldn't be seen as a replacement for working with your therapist or taking prescribed medication. Rather, use it as a supplemental tool to enhance your therapeutic experience. Whether your therapist recommended this book or you've discovered it yourself, it's a good idea to let your therapist know that you have this workbook and when you plan to start using it.

THE 10 COGNITIVE DISTORTIONS

Being familiar with the cognitive distortions is integral to work you are doing in this workbook. You will need to know these cognitive distortions to practice cognitive reframing, which involves catching, challenging, and changing your thoughts about something. Cognitive reframing modifies your emotional reactions toward a trigger and broadens the range of actions available that you can take in response to it. You may want to flag this page or take a snapshot of it so that you can easily refer to the cognitive distortions as you do the exercises. (You can also find an abbreviated list in the back of the book on page 172.) The 10 cognitive distortions we have decided to focus on are:

1. **All-or-nothing thinking (aka black-and-white thinking).** When this cognitive distortion is present, you find yourself using words like "always," "everything," or "never." Let's say your car breaks down on your way to a meeting. You may say something like, "This *always* happens to me" or "*Everything* is messed up" or "Things *never* go my way!" It's important to realize that there are shades of gray. Likely, your car doesn't always break down and sometimes things do go your way. Yes, a broken-down car is messed up, but that doesn't mean everything is.

2. **Overgeneralization.** With this cognitive distortion, you see one event as part of a never-ending pattern. In so doing, you may view a situation as hopeless because one thing goes wrong. For example, you do poorly on an exam in a class, so you think, "I'm going to fail this class." Or one of your coworkers at your new job is unkind to you, so you think all your coworkers will behave the same way.

3. **Mental filtering.** When your mental filter is on, you ignore all the good things that are happening and focus only on the bad stuff. Perhaps you wrote a really good paper for class, but your professor circled a few typos. You focus on the errors rather than the couple of positive comments the professor also made.

4. **Disqualifying the positive.** While this is similar to mental filtering in that you only focus on the negatives, you are actively disqualifying the positive as not counting or as something that isn't likely to happen again. Let's say you give a speech that goes really well, but you disqualify the positive feedback ("They were just being polite"), and therefore the next time you give a speech you don't count this last experience, so you think you'll forget your lines or draw a blank.

5. **Jumping to conclusions.** This is when you conclude without evidence that something negative is happening. Let's say your boss asks to meet with you and you predict that you're going to get reprimanded for a mistake or get fired. Perhaps you don't hear from someone when they said they'd contact you, and you conclude they are mad at you. *Fortune telling* and *mind reading* are the two main subtypes of jumping to conclusions. Fortune telling is when you make a negative prediction about the future and treat it as a fact, and mind reading is when you believe you know what the other person is thinking without asking them.

6. **Magnification or minimization.** An example of magnification is when you host a dinner party and forget that one of your guests is a vegetarian. You blow up the significance of that one oversight and conclude that it ruined your gathering. With minimization, you might look at your accomplishments and think, "Well, sure, anyone could do that."

7. **Emotional reasoning.** Here, you assume that because you feel an emotion intensely, the thoughts associated with the emotion must be true. For example, if you have a fight with a friend and feel very angry or sad, you may be convinced that the friendship is over. As another example, sometimes when people feel very depressed, they believe they are a bad person. And many people who feel

very anxious on a plane believe that must mean they are in danger (e.g., the plane is going to crash).

8. **"Should" statements.** With this cognitive distortion, you are holding yourself to certain, often rigid, rules. For example, "I should have cleaned the house better" or "I should have aced this test" or "I should be a better friend."

9. **Labeling and mislabeling.** When you use negative labels on yourself or others, you are defining yourself or them in a limited way. Let's say you forgot to call a friend back. You think, "I'm a terrible friend." Or remember that coworker who was unkind to you? You think, "That guy is a nasty jerk."

10. **Personalization.** Even though you may not have any control over a situation, when you personalize, you make yourself to blame. For example, if someone around you is upset, you conclude that you must have done something to upset them.

KEEP A THOUGHT RECORD

A thought record is one of the key tools of CBT. It will help you become more aware of and clearer about the statements you make to yourself, moment to moment, that you're not always attuned to. Your thought record will help you improve your understanding of how those thoughts can influence how you feel and what you do or don't do.

Time: 15 minutes

Format: Written exercise

Instructions: The following chart has three columns, labeled "Automatic Thought," "Cognitive Distortion(s)," and "Rational Thought." In the first column, write down a problematic thought you are having. Look at the descriptions of the cognitive distortions in the previous section (see page 7) and identify which might be at play within that thought, and write that in the second column in order to challenge it. Next, *reframe* (i.e., change) the thought into a more rational thought in the third column. Look at the example provided for assistance. The more you work through this book, the clearer this exercise will become, so revisit it often!

AUTOMATIC THOUGHT	COGNITIVE DISTORTION(S)	RATIONAL THOUGHT
I thought my public speech went well because of the cheering and applause. The next day I checked social media, and there was a mean comment on the video of me speaking. I guess the speech wasn't any good.	Mental filtering Disqualifying the positive All-or-nothing thinking Magnification	The speech was well received by almost everyone! I know this because of the applause and positive reaction of the audience after I finished speaking. As for the one negative comment online, you can't please everyone. Just because one person didn't like my speech, it doesn't negate all the praise I received from the crowd.

AUTOMATIC THOUGHT	COGNITIVE DISTORTION(S)	RATIONAL THOUGHT

CHANGE TAKES PRACTICE

At first, it might feel odd to pay so much attention to your thoughts, but as time goes on, you will begin to have a greater understanding of what you are thinking, how these thoughts influence what you are doing, and how to change your thoughts and behaviors to start feeling happier and more satisfied. When you change your thoughts and behaviors into more productive ones, your feelings and your sense of self-worth can improve, too. Curbing negative automatic thoughts by identifying the cognitive distortions in them and bravely testing out your beliefs goes a long way.

The great thing about CBT is that it's a skills-based approach. You're learning tools and techniques that you can use every day. After a while, your new way of thinking and acting will seem routine. And while you can't (and shouldn't try to) *control* your thoughts, using CBT techniques allows you to better *manage* them in a variety of ways (e.g., challenge them, test them out, or even just notice and accept them).

While simple in concept, CBT is so powerful that it can change the way the brain functions. According to a study at the University Hospital of Psychiatry Zurich, patients with social anxiety were given a 10-week CBT treatment. Using magnetic resonance imaging, the subjects' brains were examined before and after a course of CBT. The researchers found that the better the outcome for the patient, the stronger the brain changes that were observed. They were also able to demonstrate that the brain areas involved in processing emotions were more interconnected after the treatment. Thus, they concluded, "Psychotherapy normalizes brain changes associated with social anxiety disorder." According to the Beck Institute, thousands of research studies show how effective CBT is for people struggling with depression, anxiety, addiction issues, and much more. The research stands for itself. CBT has been around for more than 50 years now, and it continues to be applied to new areas to help people feel better about themselves.

Tips for Best Practices

When you learn a new skill, it's crucial to practice it. That's the case for learning the skills taught in CBT. Remember, there are many components to CBT. It will take you some time to learn the techniques found in each component. The more you practice, the better you will become at using them, until they become second nature to you.

You probably don't need to make major changes in the way you live. And even if you do, we encourage you to think of big changes as nothing more than a series of little changes that are strung together over time. There are many little things you can do

each day to develop these skills and keep the skills sharp. Just doing these little things can have a major impact on your life. And once you learn the skills, you will always have the tools with you—as long as you keep practicing. Therefore, when you have a challenging situation in front of you in the future, you can better handle it by tapping into the CBT tool kit you have built in your mind. The following are some tips for practicing CBT daily.

BE FLEXIBLE IN HOW YOU THINK

Allow yourself to see the middle ground. If you find yourself using words like "always," "never," "nothing," "every time," "everyone," and "forever," stop yourself; these are extreme words that foster *all-or-nothing thinking*. If you think things will "always" be a certain way, it's likely linked to why you feel unhappy or dissatisfied. This is a fatalistic way of viewing the world. Instead of saying, "I always feel down," you can change that statement to "I often feel down" or "I feel down right now." Consider alternative thoughts. Before deciding the way you think about something is a fact, consider how other people might view the situation. Then consider the costs and benefits of continuing to see the situation the way you do. Being flexible in your thinking allows you to reframe your problematic thoughts into more helpful ones that you can then act on.

BE MORE MINDFUL

Sometimes you just feel bad or are having a bad day and don't know what caused it. That happens to many of us. That's why mindfulness is so important. Basically, mindfulness as a skill involves focusing your attention on the present moment and observing what's there (inside or outside you) without judging it or trying to change it. When you start to feel any uncomfortable emotion, it may be helpful just to pay attention to your emotion without judging it. You can also observe the thoughts going through your mind. What do these feelings and thoughts lead you to want to do? Remember, the skill is to simply notice without judgment. The more you observe your thoughts, feelings, and sensations without judging them, the better you'll understand the effect they can have on you and the more adept you'll be at letting the problematic ones go.

FEEL YOUR FEELINGS

Similar to being mindful, it's important to understand that all feelings—positive and negative—are real and can be useful in certain situations. Therefore, the more you learn to allow yourself to experience all emotions fully, the better able you'll be to tolerate ones

that don't feel good (often negative emotions, such as anger, sadness, anxiety, etc.) or aren't as useful in a particular situation. Ditto for sensations. The CBT exercises you'll learn can help you acknowledge and work through painful emotions and sensations. For example, when you feel anxious, don't run away from that feeling by doing something to escape it. Rather, allow yourself to experience the anxiety and work through the feeling, even if it's uncomfortable. Notice and describe the way anxiety feels in your body, but don't try to do anything about it. Just observe and see what happens. That way, you give the anxiety (or whatever you are feeling) less power over you, and you'll feel more confident in your ability to experience it in the future. Part of CBT involves accepting the way you feel in the moment. It also involves understanding that your feelings aren't permanent. The idea that feelings don't last forever can be comforting in the moment.

EMBRACE THE UNKNOWN

Many people don't do well with uncertainty. Even when you are practicing CBT, you won't know for certain how things will go after working through your negative thoughts or changing your behaviors. It's crucial to have patience with the unknown. It's okay to be anxious or afraid of what lies ahead. The important thing is to start to build a tolerance for uncertainty by facing it, rather than avoiding it. When facing uncertainty, if uncomfortable feelings arise, try to stay with them, observe, and tolerate them, and don't judge yourself for experiencing anxiety when facing uncertainty or the unknown. Keep in mind that one of the central tenets of CBT is that you can change how you feel by modifying your thoughts and actions. When you remember that you have this power, you can move forward with more confidence in what's to come.

PRACTICE SELF-COMPASSION AND SELF-ACCEPTANCE

There will be times when life is just plain hard, and we are all fallible. To live a full life means that sometimes we will make mistakes and sometimes we will be disappointed. Even practicing your CBT skills will be difficult at times, and you may become frustrated with the process. That's understandable. Remind yourself that just making the decision to try to change your thought patterns and behaviors is a worthy challenge that you've undertaken. Be gentle with yourself if you don't feel like you're getting it all right away. Like any other skill, there's a learning curve to CBT, so some days will be easier than others.

Let's say your friend is feeling down because she's falling behind in a class and feels like a failure. As her friend, you might show her compassion by saying, "Wow, that must be painful to feel like you're a failure. I'm sorry you are going through that. Is there anything I can do to help?" You aren't trying to talk her out of it. Instead, you are being

empathetic and offering her assistance if she needs it. The goal is to try to treat yourself the same way. Say the same words aloud to yourself that you'd say to a friend who is learning something new and having a hard time at it. This is what it means to have self-compassion.

DO YOUR PERSONAL BEST

Have you ever heard the saying "compare and despair"? There's no benefit to comparing yourself to others who seem to have it all together. You never really get to see the full picture of their lives or what they may be experiencing inside. And you are the only one who matters right now. You chose to take a path toward self-improvement. By picking up this workbook, you showed you want to better your mental health. The fact that you are reading it shows your dedication to self-improvement. Congratulations! That's the first step toward changing your negative thought patterns and problematic behavioral patterns. Take it step-by-step and treat this book as a learning opportunity. We're here to show you how CBT can benefit you and your daily life. All you need to do is come ready to learn. There may be times when you find practicing your CBT skills is difficult or that some of the concepts are hard to master. Remember that everything takes practice. Even if you don't get it right away, keep going.

STAY OPEN

We don't like to say "stay positive," because maybe you're going through a tough time that is realistically quite challenging. Staying positive may not be a realistic option for you at the moment and, in fact, trying to do so would invalidate your feelings. But we will say "stay open" to whatever you're feeling and thinking and to new experiences and learning new skills.

LET'S MOVE FORWARD

CBT is practical and versatile in the ways it can help you. Take a moment to think about what you'd like to learn from CBT. Maybe you want to get better at understanding your emotions. Perhaps you want to learn to deal with panic attacks. You might be struggling with a depressed mood. You might be having trouble with your self-esteem or self-acceptance. CBT can help with all these goals, and more.

Now that you have a background understanding of what CBT is and have dipped your toes in a bit, it's time to delve deeper. You will not only learn a lot about CBT but also—and more importantly—learn how it relates to your life. By the way, you can share what you are learning with your friends and family; just don't try to be their therapist. CBT has so much to offer, but you've got to want to put in the work and then stay committed to doing that work. There's no magic cure. Change will come from wanting to make change and then working hard to get it, while also staying committed to your goal when challenges inevitably arise along the way. Now, let's dive in!

GROWING SELF-ESTEEM AND SELF-ACCEPTANCE

The term "self-esteem" is used to describe a person's overall sense of self-worth. Basically, it's how much a person likes and values themselves. If you have good self-esteem, you feel confident and capable, but if you are struggling with low self-esteem, you doubt yourself and your abilities. When you work on your thoughts and actions using your CBT skills, your sense of self-esteem can increase.

Equally if not more important than liking and valuing the positive things about yourself is accepting the things about yourself that you don't necessarily like or admire and

that may not be so easily changed. While psychology once concentrated only on self-esteem, the field has evolved and integrated the concept of self-acceptance. Self-acceptance helps us be gentler with ourselves about the things in life that are more challenging to shift (e.g., our weight, the world, people in our lives, etc.) or can't be changed (e.g., our past). When you practice self-acceptance, you learn to embrace all aspects of yourself, including both your strengths and the areas you think you need to work on.

WHY WE MAY STRUGGLE WITH SELF-ESTEEM

There are many factors that contribute to who we become in the world, which directly impacts our level of self-esteem. Let's take a look at them now. Don't be discouraged if you identify with any—or all—of these factors. There are numerous ways to use CBT to work through your self-esteem issues. One is to target your inner critic, and we'll discuss that topic soon. For now, just work on becoming aware of what might be the root cause of your self-esteem issues.

Environmental Triggers

The people in your environment and what you see in the media and advertising can all affect your level of self-esteem. Perhaps you were raised in an overly critical household where virtually nothing you said or did was "good enough." Or perhaps you received a lot of critical feedback from peers, teachers, or coworkers. Maybe you fell into the trap of comparing yourself to society's "ideal" standards or other people you saw as being on a pedestal, and you criticize yourself for not meeting those standards. Criticism has a big impact on self-esteem, so we'll look at it much more deeply following this section.

Bullying

If you were the victim of bullying as a child or adolescent, those wounds can linger into adulthood and impact your self-esteem. If the bullying started in adulthood (it's a misconception that it happens only to children), it can cause you to "rewrite" your history and change how you've always seen yourself. Bullying can happen in the workplace, at school, in social settings, on the Internet ("cyberbullying"), and even at home. Bullies know how to target a person's insecurities and manipulate them. That causes the person on the receiving end of the bullying to question their sense of self and value, which leads to self-esteem issues.

Breakups and Other Types of Rejection

Breaking up with a significant other hurts, and it can be a significant blow to your self-esteem. If you are with a person for a long time, you are accustomed to receiving their love and support in whatever form it takes. When that love and support is

removed, you experience a loss and it may cause you to have negative thoughts about yourself, such as, "What's wrong with me?" and lead you to conclude that you're the reason that they no longer want to be with you. This can be true for shorter relationships as well. In more extreme circumstances like codependent relationships, one person's love and approval may feel crucial to the other person's sense of worth.

Even if the relationship (whether romantic or otherwise) is ongoing, the absence of positive feedback can affect your sense of worth. Rejection also falls into this category. Being rejected for whatever reason in any type of circumstance can be a blow to a person's self-esteem.

Identity Issues

Many people struggle with figuring out who they are and want to be in the world. If you relate, you're not alone. It could be that you're in the midst of questioning your sexual orientation or gender identity and you don't feel secure in yourself yet. Or maybe you're a part of a culture that doesn't accept you because you don't fit its "mold." Identity struggles are real and can take many forms; all can negatively impact your self-esteem.

Lack of Support System

We all need people with whom to share both the good times and the bad. Some support systems are built in, like large, loving families, for instance. Sometimes support systems must be built from the ground up, which takes time and energy. They're an investment of an emotional nature, but they really pay off when they function well. Not having any people in your life who build you up by noticing and appreciating what's great about you and supporting you in tough times could contribute to low self-esteem.

Biological Factors

According to a study published in *Psychological Medicine* in 2007, chronic self-esteem issues can have a biological component. If your parents or relatives struggled with self-esteem issues, you may be wired (i.e., genetically predisposed) to experience the world similarly. Any given situation could be interpreted in a more self-deprecating way by someone with this biological tendency when compared to someone without it.

Trauma

A history of traumatic experiences, or even a single traumatic incident, can impact a person's self-esteem. People often blame themselves for the trauma they've endured. Even though they may logically know that it wasn't their fault, they may struggle emotionally to believe it. In addition, sometimes other people's poor behavior toward a trauma victim can have a detrimental effect on that person's self-worth. If you suffered trauma and are reexperiencing symptoms of it at a level that is distressing or is interfering with your ability to function at home, at work, in school, or in life, it is crucial to seek the help of a mental health professional. This workbook can support the work you do with your therapist but cannot replace it.

CRITICISM CAN BE CONSTRUCTIVE

Criticism gets a bad rap because it is often difficult to embrace and therefore can interfere with how we feel about ourselves. It's true that some forms of criticism are harmful and abusive, but some are actually constructive and can help us improve. It's just a matter of discerning the difference between destructive and constructive criticism.

You've probably heard the term "inner critic," that voice in our head that's criticizing what we are doing or how we are doing it. It may even be criticizing who we are more generally. What you may not know is that the inner critic often means well and may be reframed into simply our attempt to look for ways we can be better. The problem is that with some mental health challenges, that voice can be *very* loud. The other problem is that we can't get rid of the inner critic. It will be a voice we must contend with for our entire lives. So the best approach is to be aware of it, learn to live with it, take what it says with a healthy dose of skepticism, and reframe its critical statements into *suggestions* for ways in which we can grow.

Whether the criticism is coming from someone else or from your inner critic, it's easy to focus and dwell on it to the point that it stops you in your tracks. This is where cognitive reframing comes in. First, distance yourself from criticism by mindfully listening to it without judgment; listen dispassionately. Then, try to find the grain of truth in it, and lastly, reframe it to something constructive. Not all criticism is completely off base, so if you don't take it personally, it can help you learn about yourself and grow. For example, let's say you're a writer and you submit an article to a publication. The editor gets back to you and says they like your writing, but the article has sentences that are

too long and overly descriptive. You could take that as a criticism and ignore it, or you could use it as an opportunity to reexamine your writing style and see if you can tweak it for the next time you submit a piece. Not all criticism is a bad thing, and it can be an opportunity for growth. The following exercises can help.

HEAR AND RESPOND TO YOUR INNER CRITIC

Your inner critic is a sometimes well-meaning part of your mind that wants the best for you. It offers advice or feedback on your character or the actions you take. However, sometimes it doesn't have the most sensitive or tactful approach. This exercise helps you take your power back and observe how your inner critic is actually trying to help.

Time: 15 to 20 minutes

Format: Observation and written exercise

Instructions: Respond to the following prompts to discover how your inner critic is trying to help you:

1. Sit quietly for a moment and listen. Now, for the next five minutes, list all the thoughts your inner critic is throwing at you. They may come at you rapid-fire. Allow yourself to write down these thoughts without judging them or trying to stop them. These are *automatic thoughts*. (Some examples of automatic thoughts, which are not necessarily yours, might include criticisms like, "I'm bad with money," "I'm not a good friend," and "I'm a lazy parent.")

_____

_____

_____

_____

_____

_____

_____

_____

_____

_____

_____

2. Now review your list. These statements may sound pretty harsh. On the surface, it may seem like your inner critic is being cruel. Circle just three of the thoughts to work with for now. We'll call these your "hot" thoughts. Pick the three that seem to be the most bothersome of the bunch.

3. Look at these three hot thoughts without judging them and, in the spaces provided, try to reframe them so that they are helpful. To help you here, let's look at the three examples of automatic thoughts from step 1, with the understanding that these may not be your thoughts:

    → "I'm bad with money." The inner critic is trying to tell you that you have some financial issues that need to be worked on. You can reframe this critical statement of "I'm bad with money" to "I need help with money management." You may then choose to reach out to a financial advisor or ask someone you trust for help.

    → "I'm not a good friend." Here, your inner critic is telling you to pay attention to your friendships and work on them. By _labeling_ yourself a "bad friend," you are learning that you care about improving your friendships. Now you can examine ways to show up for your friends while being gentle with yourself and recognizing that no friendship is perfect. You may choose to write down the name of one friend and think of something nice you can do for them. Maybe you'll send a text or call them and ask how they're doing.

    → "I'm a lazy parent." Being a parent is difficult. Your inner critic recognizes that being a parent requires a lot of hard work. There's a difference between being lazy and feeling tired. All parents get tired. You are calling yourself lazy because you care. That makes you a good parent. You may choose to ask yourself, "What small thing can I do to show I care, despite feeling tired?"

Thought 1: _____

Reframe: _____

Thought 2: _____

Reframe: _____

Thought 3: _____

Reframe: _____

Do you see now how your inner critic might actually be trying to help? The way it's communicating is harsh, but the message is one of encouragement to better yourself. We all have challenges in life and things that we can get better at, and that's what the inner critic is trying to show us. You're not bad with money, a bad friend, or a lazy parent. But at the same time, there are always ways you can seek to feel better about yourself and improve your relationships.

PRACTICE SELF-APPRECIATION

One way to redirect your inner critic is to focus on what you appreciate and value about yourself. Think of it as an emotional seesaw: the more you appreciate who you are, the less your critical thoughts can weigh you down. This doesn't mean you won't critique aspects of yourself or your actions; it just means that your criticisms will feel less personal and more like suggestions than declarations. Part of building self-worth is accepting and appreciating who you are and what you have.

Time: 10 minutes

Format: Written exercise

Instructions: Respond to the following prompts:

List five things you like about yourself or have in your life; these are things you are grateful for. It could be as simple as "I like my eyes." You could also appreciate a quality about yourself, such as "I'm kind to others."

1. _____

2. _____

3. _____

4. _____

5. _____

List all the reasons you appreciate these things about yourself. For example, why do you like your eyes? Are they a particular color you like; do you have great vision; are they deep or inviting? What makes you feel good about being kind to others? Is it because you're kind to children or the elderly or animals or those less fortunate? Come up with all the reasons you can think of to be grateful for those five things. Note: we've included a lot of space here on purpose!

_____

_____

_____

_____

_____

_____

_____

_____

_____

_____

_____

_____

_____

_____

GIVE YOUR INNER CRITIC TIME OFF WITH ACTIVITY

A good way to deal with your inner critic is to do something other than listen to it. It's easy to be self-critical when you're less active, because sitting around leaves more opportunity for you to pay attention to your negative thoughts. The more sedentary you are, the more likely—and more often—you are to hear your thoughts. On the other hand, it's difficult to be self-critical when you're doing something active that gives you a sense of accomplishment or pleasure. Some CBT exercises have to do with changing the way you think, but the science is clear that certain types of activities can also help you feel better. This is called *behavioral activation*.

Time: 30 minutes

Format: Written exercise and behavioral activity

Instructions: Pick a time daily to fully engage in an activity that you truly enjoy, just for the pleasure of it, or that gives you a sense of accomplishment after it is done, or both! This can include things such as cooking, yoga, walking in nature, taking a nice

bath or shower, or crafting. It can also include things like cleaning, paying your bills, and doing your laundry. Whatever you choose, try to really be present in this activity, noticing how the food smells while you are cooking or how your body feels when it is holding a yoga pose or how the leaves sound when the wind blows through them. Notice how you feel after it is done. Is your motivation higher?

By engaging with valued activities in this way, you can turn your attention away from the negative chatter in your head and immerse yourself in experiences that bring meaning and pleasure to your life. You can also use the activity to fully engage in life. And once you're able to follow through on this activity, you'll feel good about yourself for having accomplished it, which will help you gain confidence and increase your self-esteem and motivation.

Respond to the following prompts:

What activity would you like to do?

Which days and times will you do this activity?

After you have engaged in the activity, make a note of how you feel here:

After you have engaged in the activity, rate your level of motivation from 0 (no motivation) to 10 (high motivation).

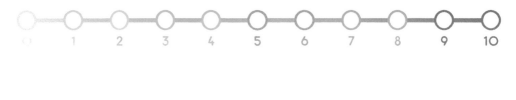

0   1   2   3   4   5   6   7   8   9   10

PRACTICE SELF-COMPASSION

We are often quick to be compassionate toward others but don't exercise the same level of concern or care with ourselves. You can build your self-esteem by practicing self-compassion. Self-compassion isn't about feeling sorry for yourself; it's about acknowledging that life can be challenging at times and that hearing constant negative feedback in your mind hurts. When you practice self-compassion, you are kind to yourself no matter what happens. Rather than disregarding your painful feelings or suppressing negative thoughts, you accept them and then choose to be good to yourself. You treat yourself as you would a good friend. Self-compassion is a way to address your need for validation. While it's always nice to get support from others, you can feel empowered when you realize that you don't need others to validate your pain when you have the tools to manage it yourself.

Time: 10 minutes

Format: Mindfulness

Instructions: You can practice this exercise wherever you are (even while walking down the street) at any point in your day when you notice a negative thought that is causing you pain.

1. Notice your negative thoughts. For example, perhaps you catch yourself thinking something like, "I hate my life. I have nothing going for me."

2. Notice how these thoughts make you feel.

3. Rather than trying to convince yourself that these thoughts are not true, practice being compassionate. Respond to the thoughts with a gentle voice either aloud or in your mind by saying something like, "Wow, that sounds painful. I'm

sorry you're hurting. You certainly have gone through a lot lately." This reminds you that your feelings are real and that life isn't easy. If you recognize how difficult certain circumstances are, it can alleviate some of the suffering.

4. Notice how you feel after each time you try this approach.

CRAFT YOUR OWN AFFIRMATIONS

If you've been feeling down for some time, you're probably accustomed to hearing repetitive, cruel thoughts in your head about your character, the world you live in, or your future. One way to combat these thoughts is to develop and use affirmations. Affirmations are statements, or mantras, that can work directly against the negative ruminations.

Time: 10 minutes

Format: Written exercise and verbal practice

Instructions: To get your attention away from your negative thoughts, use an affirmation that resonates with you and repeat it frequently when negative self-talk arises. Here's how to choose one:

Think about something simple and straightforward you would say to a friend who is having a tough time; for example, "You're doing the best you can." Then rephrase it to speak directly to yourself. Here are a few ideas:

→ I'm doing the best I can.

→ My thoughts don't determine my worth.

→ I'll just focus on what's in front of me and take it one step at a time.

→ I know these statements feel true, but feelings aren't facts.

It's essential to craft a statement that resonates with you, so play around with this a little. You can choose more than one statement that helps you cope with your specific ruminations. Try to come up with three to five affirmations, and write them here:

_____

_____

_____

Note: It might be helpful if you also write your affirmation(s) on a sticky note and put it on your bathroom mirror or make it the wallpaper on your phone, tablet, or desktop.

PUTTING AN END TO RUMINATION

Rumination is a form of perseverative thinking (repeatedly thinking about the same thing) that focuses on negative content, generally involving the past and present, that nearly always results in emotional distress and over time has a way of slowly chipping away at your self-esteem. The more you ruminate about something, whether it's how you feel about yourself or it's how you feel about something that occurred, the more powerful it feels.

One reason people ruminate about negative situations is because they think they can solve these issues by dissecting and analyzing them, even though they are in the past. Human beings are analytical creatures, and that's why rumination is appealing. However, the research is clear here: the more you ruminate, the more depressed you feel, and vice versa. Over time, rumination can also feel increasingly difficult to dispute or even control. Even worse, people who engage in rumination often become accustomed to it and don't see the powerful role it is playing in their emotional distress. However, it's possible to modify this tendency. One way is to pick and choose which thoughts you pay attention to.

(BROWSE YOUR THOUGHTS)

You are not your thoughts, and you have the power to choose whether you listen to them or not, the same way you can go into a store, browse the aisles, and *not* buy

anything. When you mindfully observe your thoughts, you can let go of and leave behind any self-critical thoughts that are not relevant or productive.

Time: 15 minutes

Format: Meditation and written exercise

Instructions: Go somewhere you can be alone, and keep this book beside you to respond to the prompts after the meditation. Get comfortable. You can sit on the floor or in a chair or even lie in bed. Choose any position that makes you feel comfortable and safe. Set a timer for five minutes.

1. Close your eyes and let your mind wander.

2. Notice the thoughts that are coming and going through your mind and picture them like clouds in the sky. These are simply automatic thoughts that you don't have control over. Some thoughts will be negative. Your inner critic may be spouting criticisms such as "You made a mistake today" or "Everyone thinks you're incompetent" or even "This exercise is a waste of time" or "She said (*fill in the blank*), so I should've said (*fill in the blank*)." Remember: it's likely your inner critic is trying to be helpful, but in a maladaptive way.

3. Without judging the contents of your thoughts, just observe them and let them be. Simply be aware of them without engaging them in any way. If you find yourself responding to them, remind yourself to just picture them like clouds in the sky, floating by at their own speed.

4. Now try to mentally sit in the space or distance between you and your thoughts. You are not your thoughts. You can mentally say, "I am separate from thoughts," or, without interpreting the thought, say, "My mind is telling me that . . ." and then observe. Simply let your thoughts be present without trying to change or judge them.

5. When the timer goes off, respond to the following prompts.

What is a self-critical thought you had during the meditation?

_____

_____

On a scale from 0 to 10, how convinced are you that this thought is true?

On a scale from 0 to 10, how skilled were you at observing this thought without engaging it?

On a scale from 0 to 10, how helpful was it to take this stance?

OUTSIDE INFLUENCES ON SELF-ESTEEM

You may find that when others criticize you or disapprove of something you've done, your self-esteem takes a blow. We can't control people expressing their criticism or disapproval from time to time, but we can control the way we receive it. Here are two exercises that can help you take outside opinions with a grain of salt, just like you would with your inner critic's feedback.

PREDICT AND TEST OUT DISAPPROVAL

If someone criticizes you or disapproves of an action you took, it doesn't mean you've done something wrong. Each person is entitled to their thoughts, feelings, and opinions, and yours are just as valid as anyone else's. But there's a distinction between *thinking* a person has taken issue with you or something you've done and their outwardly telling you this is the case. There's also a difference between someone

deliberately trying to hurt you through an unkind action and their simply not being happy with something you did, which can be a matter of perspective.

Time: 15 minutes

Format: Written exercise and behavioral activity

Instructions: In this exercise, you will engage in a behavioral experiment where you make a prediction as to how a certain action you take will be disapproved of by another person. Start with someone you know and with something small, such as being assertive about choosing a restaurant to eat at or an activity you will do together. Respond to the following prompts before trying the activity.

Choose a situation and the behavior or action you will take that you think the other person will disapprove of:

_____

_____

_____

What are you afraid will happen? Be specific.

_____

_____

_____

How will you know if it happens? It must be observable.

_____

_____

_____

When the scenario presents itself, intentionally behave the way you planned in that person's presence and then observe what happens. Gather evidence that supports or refutes your prediction. And remember to make sure your prediction is specific and observable. Otherwise, the only way to know for certain if that person disapproves of an action you took is to ask.

ACKNOWLEDGE AND EVALUATE CRITICISM

People often make assumptions about who we are and how we behave. Just because somebody says or thinks something about you doesn't make it true. A person could say, "You're purple." The statement is only their perception of you. There are instances when someone may say something that hurts you, but it's due to their own problems. When you know your own self-worth and value who you are and what *is* true about you, that type of criticism can roll right off. But do try to be open to criticism in general to see if it contains any truth, the way you did in the exercise on page 24 with your inner critic's feedback.

Time: 15 minutes

Format: Written exercise

Instructions: This exercise teaches you to acknowledge criticism you receive from outside sources and evaluate whether there's any truth to it. It helps you differentiate between how you see yourself and the way others may see you. Doing this also helps ground you in what you know to be true about yourself and helps you see when something is clearly the other person's issue. Respond to the following prompts:

Recall an instance when someone criticized you but their criticism felt off base or didn't resonate with your understanding of the situation. Where did this take place? Who was the person and what did they say to you? Summarize it here:

_____

_____

_____

What did you think of their criticism? What was your emotional reaction to it? Since you are no longer in the middle of the situation, you can better assess the reality of the situation and the accuracy of your thoughts about it.

_____

_____

_____

How do you think this person sees you? Does this ring true for you? Why or why not?

_____

_____

_____

Is there anything productive you can take from this person's criticism? If so, what is it?

_____

_____

_____

DISCERN FACT FROM OPINION

There's a clear difference between fact and opinion. A fact is "There are stars in space," while an opinion is "The stars in space are beautiful." When someone says something about you or something you've done, and even when you say something about yourself, try to separate fact from opinion to start noticing the difference. When you can separate the facts from the opinions, you can decide whether or not the facts jibe with your understanding of the situation, whether you agree with the opinions, and if there's something you want to do about it. This can increase your self-confidence in a variety of situations, because you're clear on what needs to happen next.

Time: 5 to 10 minutes

Format: Written exercise

Instructions: The following chart contains three columns: "Statement," "Fact," and "Opinion." Think about a recent encounter you had with someone where you felt criticized and fill in the statement column with what they said to you. Then decide whether or not those statements were based on fact or opinion and make a check mark in the appropriate box. Here's a work-related example to get you started:

STATEMENT	FACT	OPINION
You were two days late with your report.	✓	
You're really screwing up.		✓
I'm going to write you up.	✓	

In this case, you know that you were late with your report and there would be consequences. However, the boss's comment that you're screwing up is your boss's opinion. You do not have to take anyone's opinion to heart and make it your own. Here, you might decide to up your game at work to avoid another late report.

Now it's your turn:

STATEMENT	FACT	OPINION

STATEMENT	FACT	OPINION

TIP: What's great about this exercise is that you can also use it for the conversations you have with yourself. Discerning fact from opinion is a great way to see what assumptions you're making about yourself and reframe them into more constructive feedback that helps you grow.

EMBRACING PERSONAL GROWTH

If you feel stuck in your negative thinking, you know that's an upsetting space to be in. When you're feeling down about yourself, it's natural to reach out for support, but it's not up to your loved ones to make emotional changes for you. Personal growth requires motivation to reach your goals, but it's a bit of a catch-22, because those pervasive and disruptive thoughts may be interfering with your motivation. Remember that even though we can't prevent thoughts from happening, we do have the power to decide what to do with them. So, rest assured, once you're able to reframe your negative thinking patterns, the motivation you may feel you are lacking will appear.

The more you practice CBT, the better you will become at deciding what to do with negative thoughts and directing your attention to the thoughts that will help you rather than hurt you. When you start feeling better, your motivation will increase and so will your confidence. You're growing as a person, and that's a beautiful thing. Of course, everyone has strengths and weaknesses. It's all about how you approach the improvements you want to make. You don't need to criticize or punish yourself because you have been facing a challenging time.

With the CBT skills you are developing, you will feel better equipped to handle what life throws at you, because you will have greater self-confidence as well as greater self-acceptance. You will find that your sense of self is clearer and you're not taking things as personally. You will discover that you're more motivated and committed to putting your time and energy into things that bring meaning to your life. Once you're able to clear away the negative thought patterns, you will discover what's meaningful to you, because you'll have more control over what you pay attention to and what you leave behind. That is one of the most powerful feelings you can experience: autonomy over your thoughts, feelings, and actions. That's personal growth.

MAKE A GRATITUDE LIST

When your self-esteem needs a boost, bringing to mind what you are grateful for can go a long way toward helping you feel better about yourself and your life. Focusing on the good can also improve your mood and motivation. This isn't about convincing yourself that everything's great but about recognizing that there are some great things, no matter how small, that you can appreciate and be thankful for in your day, each and every day.

Time: 10 minutes

Format: Written exercise

Instructions: List three things you are grateful for today:

1. _____

2. _____

3. _____

Even if you had a bad day, you can still find things to appreciate about it. Maybe you had your favorite muffin for breakfast or engaged in a nice conversation with someone while completing an errand. If it feels like nothing positive happened during your day, try to find some small thing, even if it's just that the sun came out. It's not easy at times,

but the more you can identify some small positive things, the stronger your gratitude muscle becomes.

If all else fails, think about a recent day when some good things happened or anticipate the good things you can look forward to the next day. Close your eyes, remember or envision that day, and then list those three things.

ACTIVATE YOURSELF

In the same way that it's important to give your inner critic time off with activity (see page 24), when you're trying to improve your self-esteem, it's especially important to do things that make you feel good about yourself, including self-care activities. When you engage in activities you find pleasurable or that give you a sense of accomplishment, your mood improves, which fosters more positive thoughts. It may take some time for improvements to kick in if you've been down for a while, but if you keep at it, you can stack the deck to increase your odds of feeling better in the long term.

Time: 15 to 30 minutes

Format: Written exercise and activity

Instructions: List five to seven activities that give you a sense of pleasure when you do them (or that you enjoyed in the past) or a sense of accomplishment after you do them (or after you did them in the past). Next to each of these activities, jot down why that particular activity brings you a sense of pleasure or mastery.

1. _____ brings me a sense of pleasure/mastery because

_____ .

2. _____ brings me a sense of pleasure/mastery because

_____ .

3. _____ brings me a sense of pleasure/mastery because

_____ .

4. _____ brings me a sense of pleasure/mastery because

_____ .

5. _____ brings me a sense of pleasure/mastery because

_____ .

6. _____ brings me a sense of pleasure/mastery because

_____ .

7. _____ brings me a sense of pleasure/mastery because

_____ .

Need a little help here? Maybe you like to write in a journal, get a pedicure, take a bath, read a book, meditate, go for a run, see a friend for coffee, or make a piece of art. Perhaps you need to do some dishes, get some groceries, answer some emails, or go through some mail. These don't have to be extensive activities that take a lot of time or cost a lot of money. If you still feel stumped on ideas, do an Internet search for "behavioral activation activities list" and see what resonates.

Do at least one thing on your list each day for a week, and notice your mood during the activities and afterward.

(KEEP A SELF-ESTEEM LOG)

There are likely many things you don't notice about yourself that if you paid more attention to would help increase your self-esteem. The key to this exercise is to learn to actually look for these things, notice them, and then appreciate them. Keeping a self-esteem log gets you into the habit of doing this.

Time: 10 minutes

Format: Written exercise

Instructions: The following log includes a row for each day of the week, along with writing prompts. Each day, try to identify at least one thing you did well, one thing you enjoyed doing, and one thing you did to help someone else. (Helping someone else can be as simple as putting your used plastic in a recycling bin, which helps the environment and in turn helps others.)

MONDAY

What did I do well today? ....

I enjoyed myself when I was ....

I helped another person by ....

TUESDAY

What did I do well today? ....

I enjoyed myself when I was ....

I helped another person by ....

WEDNESDAY

What did I do well today? ....

I enjoyed myself when I was ....

I helped another person by ....

THURSDAY

What did I do well today? ....

I enjoyed myself when I was ....

I helped another person by ....

What did I do well today? ....

I enjoyed myself when I was ....

I helped another person by ....

SATURDAY

What did I do well today? ....

I enjoyed myself when I was ....

I helped another person by ....

SUNDAY

What did I do well today? ....

I enjoyed myself when I was ....

I helped another person by ....

It's crucial to find something positive to write about yourself each day in order to keep yourself in the habit of noticing these positive things. Remember, these do not need to be big things. Maybe you got to work on time, and you'll make note of that in your first entry as something you did well. Then you had a homemade sandwich you really enjoyed for lunch, and you'll make that your second entry. Later, you complimented someone on their new haircut and made them smile. Getting people to smile might also be a big help to them!

Accounting for all the little highlights of your day on paper can help you recognize that there's so much about you to appreciate!

LESSONS LEARNED

You are more familiar now with the various reasons people struggle with self-esteem, and you have probably reconsidered how you respond to criticism from your inner critic and other people. You've also had an opportunity to practice self-acceptance and self-compassion for those things that either cannot be easily changed or have happened in the past. Combined, these are critical steps toward personal growth. Great job! Flip back through this chapter and review your entries. Think about the experiences you had with each exercise. Respond to the following prompts:

Which exercises were the most helpful and why?

_____

_____

_____

Which exercises were your least favorite? Do you need to give any of them another try?

_____

_____

_____

Did you skip any exercises? Why?

_____

_____

What is the most valuable lesson you learned from this chapter?

_____

_____

_____

_____

What do you still need to work on?

_____

_____

_____

_____

What is the next action you will take and when will you take it?

_____

_____

_____

_____

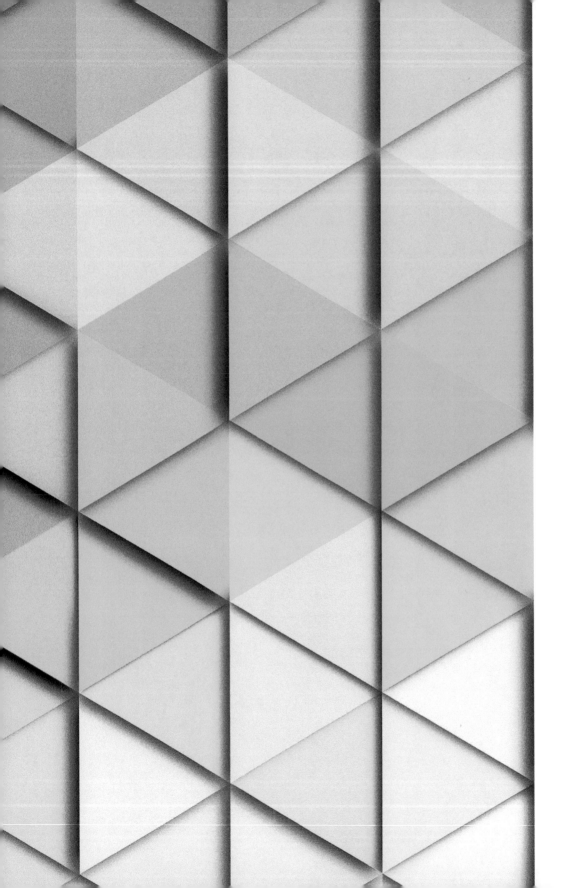

3

STRENGTHENING RELATIONSHIPS

It's essential to work on feeling good about yourself, but remember, you don't live in a vacuum. Human beings are social creatures. Even people who mainly like to spend time alone can benefit from a support system. Meaningful friendships and relationships enrich our lives and serve as a buffer against stress and low moods. It's natural to want to isolate when you don't feel good about yourself, but isolation can perpetuate the cycle of depression and enhance anxious feelings. This is why it's crucial to seek out, nurture, and maintain meaningful relationships, even when you don't feel like doing so. You don't have to look for a big group; having even one or two supportive people in your life can serve as a big buffer to emotionally challenging events in life.

Having meaningful friendships and relationships can help you feel comforted and less alone in the world. Life can be full of joyous moments, and it can bring stressful

and unpleasant moments, too. When you have meaningful relationships, they can help you cope with these stressors. During times of stress, a friend or partner can help you feel supported. That person can also be there to assist you when you slip up and to help you make better life choices. A friend or partner is a person to bounce ideas off, to get another perspective from, and to be there for you when you're feeling lost or down. Friends and partners are there to listen when you need someone to hear what's on your mind. Meaningful friendships and relationships help your mental and physical health. According to research discussed on Live Science in 2010, having good friends may actually extend your life.

The CBT exercises in this chapter can help you foster more meaningful relationships and positive interactions, and in so doing, grow emotionally as a person.

HEALTHY COMMUNICATION

Human beings often seek others to hear and understand them. Healthy relationships occur when there's respect as well as open and honest communication. When this type of emotional environment is present, it can enhance the way you feel about yourself. At times, however, all relationships can also be challenging. And, unfortunately, sometimes they can become toxic to the point of creating an abusive dynamic, which ends up hurting both individuals. Most often, however, relationships encounter a variety of less serious challenges along the way. One such challenge is not being able to speak up for yourself.

Find Your Voice

In some relationships, whether it's a friendship, family connection, or romantic partnership, it can feel challenging to speak up. One reason for this may be that you simply want to be liked. It's natural to want others to like you and to fear doing or saying things that might jeopardize their opinion of you. But a healthy relationship involves acceptance. You won't always agree with each other, but different perspectives make for good conversation. You can grow by learning from others.

Sometimes finding your voice is challenging due to low self-esteem. Revisit the exercises in chapter 2 if you struggle with this issue. When you feel more secure in who you are, embracing both your positives and negatives, you'll feel more comfortable asserting yourself, and as a result, your interpersonal relationships will improve. But perhaps you struggle with speaking up because you've been in relationships in the past with others who were cruel to you or extremely critical. It's easy to understand how it would be challenging to find your voice in future relationships. But remember, not all relationships are the same, and just because you've experienced toxic relationships before doesn't mean all your relationships are destined to be toxic. The work you are doing on yourself can prime you to be confident in selecting people to be in your life who will respect you and care about you.

There are many healthy ways to practice communicating with others. You might be nervous, and that's understandable. But think of the alternative: if you hold things inside, you will likely feel (and may in fact become) misunderstood and end up becoming resentful, regardless of what type of relationship it is. That's why it's important to express your feelings so others can hear you. Here are some helpful exercises to support good communication.

ACTIVELY LISTEN AND DEBUNK MIND READING

People often assume they know what the other person is thinking. But nobody can actually read another person's mind. Sure, you may know someone well and have a good sense of how they feel and what they're thinking based on their actions, facial expressions, or body language. But you can't *know* what they are thinking if they don't express their thoughts. This is even harder, if not impossible, over email and text because there are no nonverbal cues or tone of voice.

Time: 15 minutes

Format: Conversation and written exercise

Instructions: Ask someone close to you to work on this exercise with you (see the tip at the end of the exercise). One person will be Partner A and the other will be Partner B.

Before beginning, respond to the following prompts:

Who do you want to try this exercise with?

_____

How do you feel this technique can benefit this relationship? What changes, if any, would you like to see?

_____

_____

Now start the exercise. Partner A is completely silent while Partner B states how they are feeling. On a separate piece of paper, Partner A writes down what they heard Partner B say as well as what they think Partner B is thinking. On another piece of paper, Partner B writes down what they are actually thinking. Then compare what you each wrote.

Next, switch roles. This will help you to pay close attention to each other and likely prove that you simply cannot read the other person's mind.

TIP: Ask the person if they would like to do this exercise with you. If they say no, take a moment to write down how you feel. Are any cognitive distortions present? Remember that not everybody feels comfortable trying therapeutic exercises. Choose someone else to ask.

PRACTICE IN FRONT OF THE MIRROR

When you want to make your voice heard and to clearly communicate your thoughts with others, it's crucial to first be familiar with how your voice sounds and how your body language appears. The mirror exercise is a good way to do this. Practicing in front of a mirror can help you make adjustments and get comfortable with expressing yourself in various situations.

Time: 10 to 15 minutes

Format: Observation, verbal practice, and written exercise

Instructions:

1. Stand in front of a full-length mirror and observe your reflection. Stand straight but not rigid (try to be relaxed), keep your chin up and shoulders back (not slumped), and meet your gaze.

2. Talk to your reflection as if you were a person you want to communicate with for whatever reason. Maybe it is someone you want to stand up to and set a boundary with, or maybe it's someone you meet at a party and want to start a conversation with. Remind yourself that you are safe and can say whatever you are thinking and feeling, free of judgment, to the mirror. Remind yourself that you have a right to be heard by others.

3. Be aware of your body language as you practice expressing yourself calmly. Make adjustments as needed to your tone of voice and stance.

4. After doing the exercise, which you can practice for all sorts of scenarios, respond to the following prompts.

How did this exercise make you feel and why?

_____

_____

What were you thinking? Were there any cognitive distortions present that you can reframe?

_____

_____

What is the most powerful or most surprising thing you said to yourself during the exercise?

_____

_____

What is significant about that particular statement?

_____

_____

RELATIONSHIP BOUNDARIES

Setting and maintaining boundaries is extremely important in every type of relationship. Whether it's with a friend, partner, family member, or colleague, it's crucial to have emotional limits in place. Having boundaries is a form of self-care because you're protecting yourself against resentment and potential burnout.

You don't have to be mean or cruel when you set a boundary. For example, you can gently say, "I'm happy to help with (_fill in the blank_), but I can't help with (_fill in the blank_)," or "I like when (_fill in the blank_), but I'm not comfortable with (_fill in the blank_)." This way, you're setting reasonable expectations for the relationship up front. This can strengthen your relationships, because others will know where you stand. In fact, people who set and maintain clear boundaries are often respected for doing so.

If you don't set boundaries with people, they may not be aware of your limits and preferences. This can leave you feeling resentful and exacerbate your negative thought patterns around your relationships.

Time: 10 to 15 minutes

Format: Conversation

Instructions: Think about the people you interact with regularly and what you consider okay and not okay with regard to their behavior toward you. The things you are not okay with are the boundaries you need to set and express. Perhaps your friend pressures you to go to dance clubs late at night, but you just aren't into that scene, and she tries to get you to change your mind. You recognize her stance (she thinks it will be fun), but you disagree. It's time to stand your ground. Here's how the "stand your ground" technique works:

1. Summarize the person's feelings. (For example, "I know you really love to go dancing at clubs, and that would be fun for you.")

2. Explain that you disagree and state why you can't comply with their request. (For example, "I don't like dance clubs, and it would not be fun for me.")

3. Suggest an alternative. (For example, "I'd love to go to the movies with you. We can pick one we both want to see.") That way, you get to keep your boundary, and your friend gets the social time she wants with you.

   Respond to the following prompts:

Identify a boundary you want to set with someone and why it's important to you.

What alternative can you propose?

What negative thoughts come up for you when you think about setting a boundary? Are any cognitive distortions present? If so, try reframing them.

_____

_____

_____

_____

DEEPENING YOUR RELATIONSHIPS

If you struggle with personal or professional relationships, it may be that you need to devote some thoughtful attention to the people in your life. It's easy to get stuck in a negative thought pattern around your relationships. The following exercises will help you clear away some of the cognitive distortions around your relationships by taking an objective view of who is in your life.

ANALYZE YOUR SOCIAL NETWORK

Many people don't take stock of their relationships. This can result in unintentionally investing energy into less important relationships, when that energy could instead be directed to the people who care about us and are invested in our well-being. Maybe you've lost touch with who is and isn't close to you. Maybe you notice that you feel drained after socializing with certain people but can't explain why. It may be time to take inventory of the people in your life. Think of your social life as a dartboard with concentric circles. The bull's-eye represents your closest personal relationships. Each ring out is one step removed from those close relationships.

Time: 20 minutes

Format: Written exercise

Instructions: Take a look at the social analysis dartboard, read the descriptions of each type of relationship, then respond to the prompts.

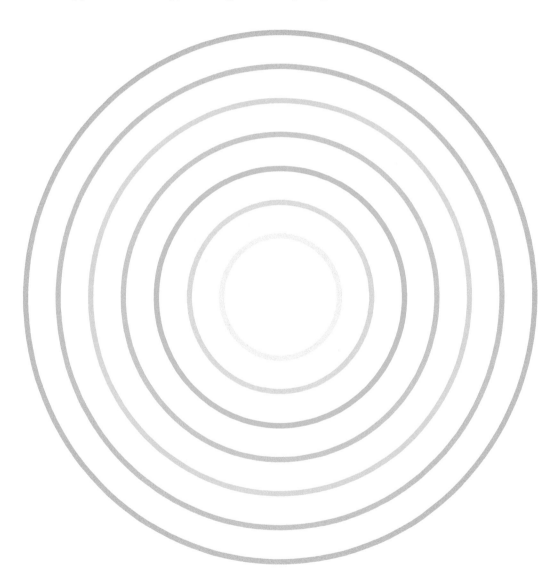

Bull's-eye: People you can be transparent with, which is a relatively small number (sometimes zero) because it requires a lot of trust.

Best friends: People you can say almost anything to, but you may still hold some personal information back from them.

Close friends: People you hang out with a lot and, depending on who is there, are willing to share some of the intimate details of your life with.

Friends: People you go to events and do activities with, but with whom you share less about the intimate details of your life.

Acquaintances: People with whom you're friendly, such as coworkers and friends of friends.

Familiar faces: People you see in the coffee shop and around town that you know and say hello to sometimes.

The rest of the world: Almost 8 billion people (as of early 2021)!

1. Take an inventory. For each ring on the dartboard, list the people in your life who fall into that category. Use their names, because it's important to be clear about who these people are. You can describe the "familiar faces" if you don't know their names.

Bull's-eye: _____

_____

Best friends: _____

_____

Close friends: _____

_____

_____

Friends: _____

_____

_____

_____

Acquaintances: _____

_____

_____

_____

Familiar faces: _____

_____

_____

_____

2. Count the number of people in each category. This is an opportunity to look at where friendships may be lacking or whether you're investing the energy in the right people. Sometimes you may feel that you don't have enough people in one ring, and other times you might think you have too many.

3. Recalibrate where you need to invest your energy in different relationships. This increases your awareness and understanding of your emotional investment and how relationships work.

4. If you've identified people in your spheres that you want to bring closer or into the inner circle, write down some ideas about how you might accomplish that. It could be as simple as starting a conversation with an acquaintance when you see them at the coffee shop. It may also require distancing yourself from people who

are "too close" (i.e., in an inner circle and requiring more energy but with little or no payoff in return).

_____

_____

MAKE AND NOTICE SMALL GESTURES

There are small gestures that we show friends, family, and others we interact with daily that tend to diminish during the course of the relationship or get waylaid when life gets busy. It's important to keep kind actions going in relationships so others know you appreciate them, and vice versa. If you notice that any relationship you value, whether it's with a friend, partner, coworker, or family member, is becoming strained or distant, dedicate some time to doing intentionally kind things for that person.

Time: 15 to 20 minutes

Format: Behavioral activity, observation, and written exercise

Instructions: Extend a deliberate kind gesture. It can be as simple as sending a text that says, "Just wanted to say hi." People love to be thought of and appreciated. Also, notice when other people extend a small gesture to you. If you notice they're being intentionally kind, say something that positively reinforces their action. For example, if they're supportive of you, extend gratitude: "I really appreciate that you called me to wish me good luck on my meeting today."

By making an effort to do this more often, you're changing your behavior to be more supportive of others by reinforcing their positive behaviors and engaging in your own.

Respond to the following prompts:

List three things you used to do for someone that you no longer do but could do again to enhance your connection.

1. _____

2. _____

3. _____

What are some actions that a person is taking or has taken in the past to be close to you? Write them down. After you've identified the actions, share them with the person by letting them know you appreciate their behavior.

_____

_____

_____

_____

DISCOVER YOUR LOVE LANGUAGE

Part of communicating with people is knowing how they receive information. This is particularly relevant when it comes to receiving love, affection, or appreciation. People express and receive love in different ways. In his book *The Five Love Languages: How to Express Heartfelt Commitment to Your Mate,* Gary Chapman talks about the five "love languages." These can apply to any type of relationship, not just romantic partners, though some demonstrations of love are only appropriate between partners. Think of this exercise as extra credit, since it would not be included in a typical round of CBT but is clearly behavioral (all things you can do) in spirit.

Time: 20 minutes

Format: Reading, conversation, and written exercise

Instructions: Sit down with someone important to you and review the descriptions of each type of love language. (You can do this on your own first, if you wish.) Take turns

sharing which love language you use to show other people you care for them. Then take turns sharing which love language makes you feel cared for. Respond to the prompts that follow. If you are having this conversation with another person, they can respond verbally.

Words of affirmation: There are people who need to hear positive words in a relationship to feel loved and appreciated. It could be as simple as saying "I love you" or telling someone they look nice. For some people, words go a long way to communicate love.

Physical touch: Some people love to be touched or held. This might be a hug, a sincere handshake, or physical intimacy.

Gifts: Some people like to receive presents to feel loved. It shows them that the other person is thinking about them.

Acts of service: There are people who feel loved when someone takes action to be helpful. Doing something for someone else can be a powerful demonstration of love.

Quality time: Some people need uninterrupted time with someone to feel loved and cared for, which is often crucial for the long-term health of a relationship. Whether you're kayaking or watching TV together, quality time strengthens relationships because it provides more time to get to know each other.

Respond to the following prompts:

What is the love language you use to show others you care for them? Is it different with different people?

_____

_____

_____

Which love language makes you feel appreciated? Again, is it different with different people?

_____

_____

_____

Which love language are you uncomfortable using? Why? Are there any cognitive distortions present?

_____

_____

_____

Which love language do you feel uncomfortable receiving? Why? Are there any cognitive distortions present?

_____

_____

_____

PRACTICE MINDFUL LISTENING

When we're having a conversation, it's very tempting to jump in and add our own thoughts without _really_ listening to what the other person is saying. One way to deepen your relationships is to listen mindfully to others when they are speaking. This means focusing your attention entirely on them while not judging what they are saying, not getting lost in your own thoughts (negative or otherwise), not _jumping to conclusions_ (mind reading), and not listening to them just to respond with your own thoughts, opinions, or advice. This takes practice, and that's what you'll have a chance to do now.

Time: 15 minutes

Format: Conversation

Instructions: The next time a friend or family member approaches you with something on their mind that they need to work out, practice listening mindfully. Listen with your complete attention to what they're saying. What kind of tone are they using? How fast are they speaking? How are they likely feeling? What does their facial

expression appear to be conveying? When they pause, give them a moment to continue. When it is clearly your turn to speak, repeat back what you heard them say and ask a question. Be curious. If they ask for your thoughts on the matter, refrain from generalizing, labeling, and judging. Check for any cognitive distortions, reframe them, and *then* respond.

TIP: If you want to practice this right away, ask someone to do this exercise with you.

TAKING OTHERS INTO CONSIDERATION

There's a difference between being intentionally selfish and not realizing that you're frequently putting your wants and desires before the needs of someone you care about. If you're intentionally selfish, that means you believe that what you want or need is more important than the other person's wants and needs. That sort of behavior can severely impact a close relationship, cause deep-seated resentment, and potentially end the relationship.

Unintentional selfishness is a different story. You simply don't realize that you've been selfish until it is brought to your attention. For example, maybe you're offering your opinion on someone's career choice. You have good intentions and want what's best for them, but part of you wants to be praised and valued for your sage advice. You don't consider that they love their current job and don't want to make a change. You're also preoccupied with receiving reassurance for being a good friend, so you're missing the fact that this person is upset by your critique. This is how unintentional selfishness can impact your relationships.

Regardless of whether your selfishness is intentional or unintentional, if your partner, close friend, or family member points out that you're not considering their needs (even if that need is to simply be accepted for who they are), it's crucial to take a step back, look at the situation, and change your behavior if you come to the conclusion that you have indeed been selfish. If you care about the relationship and want to preserve its integrity, it's time to find balance between your needs and those of your loved one. The following exercises can help.

ACCEPT OTHER PERSPECTIVES

Sometimes because you want to do something or think your approach is the best way, you might expect others to feel the same way you do. You can't imagine that they are not on the same page as you, and when they push back, you may get your feelings hurt. Insisting on your way without taking other people's ideas into consideration can be a selfish act, even if you think it's best for all involved. Instead of trying to convince them that they are wrong for thinking the way they do, try to accept things as they are, which is that they simply have a different perspective and likely have different wants and needs than you do.

Time: 20 minutes

Format: Conversation

Instructions: The next time you want to participate in a particular activity with a friend, take a certain approach at work, or make a decision that affects more than just you, instead of trying to convince the other person that what you want and need is of utmost importance, listen to their perspective and learn to accept it if it's different from yours. Follow these steps:

1. Express what you want or need and ask for their thoughts. For example, say, "I would like to go hiking with you this weekend. I need to get out in nature. What do you think?"

2. Listen to their reply. Maybe they'll agree that your suggestion sounds like a great idea. But if they don't, it's time to accept their perspective and listen to what they want and need. For example, maybe they say, "It's a bit too cold right now for hiking. I'd rather go to a movie and relax."

3. Your first inclination may be to say how stuffy movie theaters are and get angry. You might try to convince them that this weather is perfect for hiking. You might be upset with them for not meeting your need to get out in nature. None of these responses takes their perspective into account, and they could result in cognitive distortions, for example, "They think I'm crazy for wanting to go hiking in this weather" or "They don't care about my needs."

4. Your task is to radically accept things as they are right now, without judging: This person does not want to go hiking with you this weekend. There are always going to be people who don't like your ideas. It doesn't mean there's something

wrong with you or your idea. It just means the other person has a different idea of what they would enjoy. Everybody has their own perspective, including you. Perhaps they will think differently next weekend.

5. Maybe there's a middle path (i.e., alternate activity) you would both enjoy that would meet their need to relax and your need to get out in nature. If not, you can always look for another hiking partner and revisit the idea with them again in the future.

ASK "WHAT MATTERS TO YOU?"

One of the pitfalls of a relationship is assuming we know what someone needs without asking them. That falls into the cognitive distortion category of mind reading, a subtype of jumping to conclusions. We often make assumptions about others based on our own insecurities and perspectives. It's always crucial to confirm what the other person needs by asking them directly.

Time: 20 minutes

Format: Conversation

Instructions: Think about a close relationship in your life where you find yourself overly focused on making sure the other person is happy and content. You might find yourself assuming that they need certain things without asking them. Do they need you to fold their laundry, hand them their vitamins every morning, intervene in their outside relationship issues, and so on? Instead of assuming, ask clear and concise questions, with one of the best being "What matters to you?" followed closely by "How can I help you?"

By asking these questions, you will get a clear answer about what the other person needs and desires and how they would like these needs fulfilled. You can also request that they ask you these questions as well so you can begin a two-way conversation about how each of you can best support the other. No one can expect one person to satisfy all their needs and wants, but you can each enrich the other's life to the best of your ability, with emotional give-and-take at the top of the list.

ACCEPT OTHERS FOR WHO THEY ARE

When you don't accept someone for who they are, especially someone you live with, you are likely stuck in a cognitive distortion that they *should* or *shouldn't* be a certain way to satisfy your needs and desires, and you may consequently be feeling frustrated, angry, and/or resentful. People do things differently, and with any relationship, there will likely be some things you adore about your partners and friends and things some you will find unappealing. Learning to accept others for who they are (barring abusive behavior) can be a kind and considerate act.

Time: 20 minutes

Format: Conversation and observation

Instructions: What is one of your pet peeves about your partner, close friend, or family member? Maybe they stop to talk to all the neighbors when you're on a power walk together; perhaps they let their dirty laundry pile up in their closet; or maybe they like to sleep in, but you're an early riser and you always have to wait for them to get your day going. It's easy to get irritated over these things.

Instead of passing judgment—for example, thinking, "He is a blabbermouth," "She is sloppy," or "They are so lazy"—practice acceptance. Most likely they aren't being intentionally annoying or malicious. They're simply exhibiting a pattern of behavior that's different from your own. Instead of judging them for an action, simply notice it and describe it. And then let them know how you feel and, borrowing from the previous exercise, tell them what matters to you and why.

It's best to focus on your emotions. When you feel angry, hurt, or annoyed, it can be difficult not to lash out. (If you do, forgive yourself, atone if necessary, and then come back to a nonjudgmental place.) Just observe your emotions and then explain how you feel. For example, "When we're walking for exercise, I feel annoyed when you stop to chat with people. I'm out there for the exercise, not to socialize." Then give them a chance to reply. Perhaps your walking partner sees the power walk as an opportunity to socialize or they are just a naturally friendly person who can't help but engage others. Approaching the situation with acceptance and calmly sharing how you feel can make for a good conversation about how each of you can get your needs met in the relationship.

Remember to pick your battles. You may be able to learn to live with certain habits that aren't necessarily hurting the relationship, but others may be deal breakers. For example, does the other person chew "too loudly" at meals? Accept it. Are their

communication skills lacking in some way that causes frequent misunderstandings or arguments? You can still accept that they are challenged in this area while letting them know how you feel and what matters to you.

Figure out what you can accept and then practice letting the small things go. That way, when the bigger things come up, they will likely be taken more seriously.

TUNING BACK IN

Stress can drain us of the energy we would normally have to focus on our relationships, so tuning back in to people we care about is crucial when we get out of sync. There are many reasons a person may check out of a relationship, romantic or otherwise. A popular one is a miscommunication. If one person is trying to explain how they feel but no matter what they say, they don't feel heard, they may stop trying to get their needs met or to communicate their feelings.

Sometimes a person will shut down in a relationship because they don't have the emotional capacity to handle what's going on. It could be that they lack adequate coping skills and struggle to regulate their emotions. They may feel overwhelmed, anxious, hurt, or depressed about what's happening in the relationship dynamic. Instead of tuning in, they tune out so that they won't have to deal with the challenging emotions that stem from the relationship issues. This can be confusing to both parties in the relationship. If one person is withdrawing, the other person may assume they don't care enough about the relationship. Only by communicating can either of you know what the other is thinking. If either of these describes your situation, it's time to reframe any cognitive distortions and tune back in.

USE "I" STATEMENTS

An excellent way to communicate how you feel is by using an "I" statement. When you're angry or hurt, it's easy to slip into the pattern of blame, such as by saying, "You made me angry" or "You don't care about our relationship." This is an aggressive way of communicating, and it can cause the other person to feel attacked and defensive and, as a result, to tune out.

Time: 20 minutes

Format: Conversation

Instructions: Arrange a time when you can have a conversation with the person you've become out of sync with. Tell them how you feel using an "I" statement. For example, let's say your close friend always seems to rush you off the phone when you call. Sure, you could say, "You're always too busy to talk to me!" But that will likely result in a defensive response.

Instead, you can say, "I feel hurt when you don't make time to talk to me." Notice the simple format of the "I" statement: "I feel . . . when you . . ." Once you state how you feel, as a bonus, you can compliment your friend by using another "I" statement to let them know why the situation is important to you. For example, "I really value your friendship, and I miss our talks." Finally, you can also ask for their help. "What can we do to solve this problem?" Perhaps your friend will suggest that you both plan a time to talk when neither of you is busy.

This keeps the solution process collaborative, rather than blaming anyone for the problem. "I" statements, plus paying the other person a compliment and then asking for help, can in turn help each person in the relationship learn to own their feelings, listen to each other, and work together to solve relationship problems.

REFRAME THE FOUR HORSEMEN

Communication is an integral part of relationships. When you can learn to communicate effectively and show that you care about the other person's feelings, you can get back on the same page with the people you care about. The Gottman Institute uses the four horsemen (i.e., the four horsemen of the apocalypse depicting end times in the Christian tradition) as a metaphor to describe communication styles that, according to their research, can predict the end of a relationship. These communication styles are criticism, contempt, defensiveness, and stonewalling. If your impulse is to engage

in these behaviors in your relationships, then your relationships are likely in trouble. Fortunately, you can apply these principles below to any type of relationship.

Time: 20 minutes

Format: Written exercise

Instructions: Read through the descriptions of the four horsemen and then respond to the prompts.

THE FOUR HORSEMEN

Criticism: Critiquing the other person's behavior or character—for example, "I don't like the way you clean the kitchen. Why can't you do it right?"

Contempt: Name-calling, sarcasm, mocking, or mimicking the other person—for example, "You're so lazy."

Defensiveness: Responding defensively to a comment—for example, "What do you mean?! How was I supposed to know about that?!"

Stonewalling: When one person deliberately ignores the other to be mean. This is the cruelest of the horsemen.

Now think about a recent disagreement and how you behaved. Respond to the following prompts:

Were any of the four horsemen present? If so, which one(s)?

_____

_____

Ask yourself, "What emotion was the disagreement triggering in me and why?" There's a reason you felt whatever you felt. Try to figure out what the reason was. Next, note whether any cognitive distortions were present and see if you can reframe your thoughts.

_____

_____

_____

_____

_____

Jot down a few "I" statements you could have used to communicate how you felt at the time.

_____

_____

_____

_____

In the future, if you catch yourself engaging in any of these behaviors, reframe your thoughts to eliminate the cognitive distortions and reframe your response so that you own your feelings by using "I" statements and asking for help.

STRIVE FOR BALANCE IN RELATIONSHIPS

It's common for a take-charge person to seem like they have control in a relationship dynamic; it could be your spouse, your best friend, a trainer, or a boss. The reality is that no one has (or should strive to have) true control over another person. We each can decide what actions we take or don't take. In any type of relationship, it's important to ask how a person feels before making a choice that affects both of you. You can also set the boundary that the other person check with you before making a decision on your behalf.

With that said, there's a difference between a take-charge person and an overly controlling one. **If your partner isn't allowing you to socialize, is controlling your**

finances, or is being sexually, physically, or emotionally abusive, reach out to the National Domestic Violence hotline: 800-799-SAFE (7233). Abuse aside, it's possible to change the dynamics in any type of relationship so that the relationship feels more balanced. Each person should be allowed to make choices for themselves. Think about what matters to you and express your wants and needs in the context of the relationship, keeping in mind that different types of relationships fulfill different wants and needs.

KNOW WHAT TO EXPECT

Sometimes it is hard to know what to expect from and how to interact with people in different types of relationships. It is easy to fall into the trap of mistaking your boss, coworkers, employees, teachers, students, and so on for friends. While some workplaces foster that kind of environment, in most circumstances, the people you do business with aren't necessarily your friends. Likewise, your friends are not your significant other, and your significant other is not your boss, student, or teacher. Each type of relationship has different roles and expectations that inform how you behave in the relationship.

Time: 20 minutes

Format: Written exercise

Instructions: Pick a relationship that feels unbalanced. Look back at the social analysis exercise on page 56 and respond to the following prompts:

1. Ask yourself, "Who is this person to me?" Let's use your boss, for example. Because you report to them, it's natural for the relationship to be somewhat unbalanced in power. You can't expect your boss to be as sympathetic as your best friend when you want to go home early to take your sick dog to the vet. In fact, your boss might give you an unsympathetic response, leaving you feeling just as bad about their behavior as you do about your sick dog.

2. What rules are you applying to this person? Are they different from or the same as the rules you would apply to other people? Do you expect your coworkers to listen to you the way you expect your partner or friend to when you complain to them about your boss's attitude?

3. Do you feel your relationship needs to be more balanced? How can you express that to the other person? Remember to use "I" statements. In the case of your boss, you might say, "I feel upset that you give me a hard time when I ask for time off to take care of personal things. What can we do to ensure we have productive discussions going forward in which both of our needs are met?"

4. Are you personalizing the other person's response? We don't always get insight into every person's inner world. Maybe your boss was grumpy for reasons that didn't involve you. Try not to take their behavior personally, and ask yourself what else might be going on with them. How can you reframe cognitive distortions that might be at play in the relationship you're looking at?

FACE RELATIONSHIP FEARS

If you feel as if your relationship with someone is unbalanced, it may be because you have some fear around it. That fear may be giving the other person control over you even if they don't realize it. Or it may be a fear of letting someone get close to you. We all have fears, but they don't have to sabotage our relationships. This exercise helps you identify your fears and learn to face them so that your relationship feels like a two-way street that both people can travel on, sometimes together and sometimes in opposite directions.

Time: 10 to 15 minutes

Format: Written exercise

Instructions: While the feeling of fear may be real, the thoughts are worth examining so you can examine the legitimacy of your fears and then choose whether or not to take steps to face what scares you. Respond to the following prompts:

What is your fear around this relationship?

_____

_____

Where might this fear come from?

_____

_____

What thoughts are connected to the fear?

_____

_____

What cognitive distortions might be present in the thoughts?

_____

_____

What is the worst thing that could happen?

_____

_____

Is that outcome likely? Why or why not?

_____

_____

If the worst thing happened, what could you do to cope?

_____

_____

What is the best thing that could happen?

_____

_____

Is that outcome likely? Why or why not?

_____

_____

What is the most realistic outcome?

_____

_____

What action can you take to help yourself?

_____

_____

What would you tell a friend with a similar fear?

_____

_____

After doing this simple but empowering exercise, you may find that your fear around this relationship isn't as pronounced is it once seemed. When you're less afraid, you can meet the other person in the relationship with more confidence, which will help balance things out. If you notice that you're constantly in fear in your relationships, you might want to speak with a therapist, who can provide you with additional guidance and skills to work through your specific fears.

DON'T CHECK IN

People engage in checking-in behaviors to reassure themselves in uncertain situations. Intolerance of uncertainty is a common factor across all forms of anxiety, and therefore building a tolerance for uncertainty is a central aspect of many CBT treatments. Ironically, sometimes checking in too much impacts our relationships in negative ways, causing imbalance in the relationship. If we are constantly checking in, the other person will eventually get tired of being expected to reassure us, and the relationship therefore becomes strained and maybe one-sided. Curbing our checking-in behaviors

means we need to tolerate uncertainty and refocus our attention on other areas of our lives.

Time: 10 minutes

Format: Written exercise

Instructions: Think about the relationships in your life where you are constantly checking in with the other person to make sure everything is okay. This might be with a significant other or perhaps a best friend or roommate. Perhaps you are checking in because you don't trust them due to some past behavior, or maybe you are worried that there's a problem in the relationship. Whatever the case may be, trust is an integral part of a relationship. Without trust, a relationship will be unbalanced. Open communication is important to start rebuilding trust.

Let's look at some common scenarios where you might want to check in. Think about what your impulse might be in that scenario and what you could do instead. Examples have been provided.

Situation: Your friend told you they need to work late and will call you later.

Your impulse to check in: Text or call to ask exactly when they will be calling so you can plan your time around it.

Alternative response: Give your friend space to do their work and don't wait for the phone call. Do something else. If the call comes in when you're free, great! If not, you can call them back.

Situation: A family member is on the phone, but you don't know who they are talking to.

Your impulse to check in: Ask who they're talking to while they are in the middle of their conversation.

Alternative response: Step away from where they are talking; perhaps go for a walk or make a call of your own.

Situation: You've been cheated on in the past and now you are in a new relationship but worry the same thing will happen.

Your impulse to check in: When they're out of the room, check their phone for text messages or phone numbers on their call history that you don't recognize.

Alternative response: Leave the phone where it is. Go into the room where your new partner is and have a conversation with them about something you find interesting or something that's been on your mind. Building trust takes time and requires both partners' efforts, but it's worth it.

Now think of a situation in a close relationship where your impulse is to check in and describe it here:

_____

_____

_____

_____

What is an alternative response you could try?

_____

_____

_____

_____

LESSONS LEARNED

As you have now learned, the cornerstone of strong, healthy relationships is communication, which includes listening and asserting. If you've struggled to find your voice, assert yourself, or set boundaries, you now have workable strategies to practice. When you know what to expect from people (and vice versa) and show them you care, you are on your way to deepening the relationships that matter to you and accepting people for who they are—quirks and all. If a relationship falls off course or seems off-balance, you have strategies to get in sync. Flip back through this chapter and review your entries. Think about the experiences you had with each exercise. Respond to the following prompts:

Which exercises were the most helpful and why?

_____

_____

Which exercises were your least favorite? Do you need to give any of them another try?

_____

_____

Did you skip any exercises? Why?

_____

_____

What is the most valuable lesson you learned from this chapter?

_____

_____

_____

_____

What do you still need to work on?

_____

_____

_____

_____

What is the next action you will take and when will you take it?

_____

_____

_____

_____

4

MANAGING STRESS, ANXIETY, AND ANGER

Stress, anxiety, and anger are all normal parts of life on occasion, but when they start to feel overwhelming or interfere with your day, week, month, or year, practicing CBT skills can help. These three emotions are grouped together because they often occur alongside one another, but they don't have to coexist. You can feel stressed without feeling anxious or angry, and you can feel angry without feeling stressed or anxious. Let's take a look at each of these emotions in this chapter and see how you can go about weeding out the cognitive distortions that may be coming up and get a better handle on managing them. The better able you are to manage them, the more confident you will feel about your emotional awareness and how you want to behave in life.

MANAGING STRESS

Stress can take an emotional toll on us, causing us to feel the gamut of bodily sensations, and it can impact other areas of our lives, such as eating and sleeping, attention and concentration, and interpersonal relationships. While it's often quite obvious (to you and others) when you're stressed, sometimes it's hard to notice that you're feeling stressed, which may lead to conflicts with the people close to you. Later, you may regret your words or actions.

Often when we are stressed we tend to feel overwhelmed and think the worst. Maybe you're worried that you can't handle all your must-dos and start to *catastrophize*. Perhaps you've been taking a lot of days off from work to deal with family issues and you're trying to catch up on your work in the evening while taking care of your kids and other household chores, and you're behind on getting your work presentation done. Suddenly, you find yourself thinking the family issues are never going to get better, you're going to get fired from your job, your kids are going to hate you, and your home is going to fall apart. This distorted thinking is connected to your stress. Fortunately, by using the CBT skills in this chapter, you can take steps to calm yourself, as well as correct any cognitive distortions, in order to better see the reality of the situation.

MEDITATE ON STRESS

When you are stressed, it can feel overwhelming. You can also become so focused on your bodily sensations that you lose focus on who is around you and what you need to do. Stress can also make us feel more tense and irritable, which in turn can cause us to act out and say or do things that we didn't mean to say or do. You may not know how to handle these emotions yet. That's okay, and you don't have to know what to do at that moment. This exercise can help you begin to cope when your stress level feels out of control.

Time: 20 minutes

Format: Meditation and observation

Instructions: Take some time to be quiet with your stressful feelings and just let them be. All you need to do is take a seat, close your eyes, and focus on your breathing.

1. Sit in a comfortable position and close your eyes.

2. Take four deep breaths in through your nose, and breathe out through your mouth.

3. Observe where you feel the stress in your body. Stress is often experienced as a feeling of tension in certain parts of your body.

4. Take four deep breaths in through your nose, and breathe out through your mouth.

5. Let your thoughts wander.

6. Visualize the thoughts you're having as clouds floating by in the sky.

7. Take four deep breaths in through your nose, and breathe out through your mouth.

8. Reobserve where you feel the stress in your body.

9. Repeat steps 2 through 8.

10. After 20 minutes, the stress may not be completely gone, but you will likely feel a little calmer and more grounded.

Respond to the following prompts:

Where did you feel the stress in your body?

_____

_____

_____

What thoughts did you notice?

_____

_____

_____

Did letting go of your thoughts have a calming effect on you? If so, why?

_____

_____

_____

Did letting go of your physical sensations have a calming effect on you? If so, why?

_____

_____

_____

PRACTICE 5-5-5 BREATHING

Paced breathing (slow, deep, diaphragmatic breathing) is an underrated form of self-regulation that helps the body get back to a place of balance by reducing nervous system activity and facilitating the relaxation response. When your body is more relaxed, it's easier to see things clearly. As you breathe and your body relaxes, it may become clear to you that some of your stressful thoughts contain cognitive distortions, which you can reframe afterward.

Time: 10 to 15 minutes

Format: Activity

Instructions: Sit comfortably in a chair, on the floor, or wherever you feel most at ease. Inhale while slowly counting to five in your mind. Exhale, again while slowly counting to five. Wait five seconds and then repeat the process for the designated time.

While you're breathing, you will feel your body start to relax. Stressful thoughts may race through your mind; after all, when you began this exercise you were feeling

stressed. Notice the thoughts but remind yourself that you don't need to do anything. Your job here is simply to breathe.

IDENTIFY STRESS TRIGGERS

Sometimes it isn't something big that stresses us out, but rather lots of little things coming together at the same time. Suddenly you feel what you can only describe as "stressed out." There's a lot going on, much of it your ordinary everyday stuff. But now you've hit a tipping point, and you're not sure what got you there. Take some time to identify your stress triggers. It could be that you're putting more pressure on yourself than you need to.

Time: 15 minutes

Format: Written exercise

Instructions: The next time you tell yourself, "I'm so stressed," stop what you're doing and respond to the following prompts:

What led up to the situation? How were you feeling right before you told yourself how stressed you are? What were you thinking just before you made that comment? For example, perhaps you were feeling on edge and a thought came to you, such as "I'll never get this done in five hours."

_____

_____

_____

What triggered those thoughts? Maybe the task requires more than five hours, but you are pressuring yourself to stick with that time frame.

_____

_____

What beliefs did you have that caused your stress to be triggered? Perhaps it was "I'll have let everyone down if I don't complete this" or "I'm a total failure" or "I never finish anything on time."

_____

_____

_____

Identify any cognitive distortions in these beliefs.

_____

_____

_____

Try to come up with a more balanced way of thinking. What will really happen if you don't complete the project in five hours?

_____

_____

_____

MANAGING ANXIETY

Anxiety is a common emotion that many people struggle with, but there's a difference between being chronically anxious at a clinical level and experiencing feelings of anxiety less intensely or more occasionally. Anxiety is the emotion associated with a perceived threat. If a person believes they are facing danger, their body responds by

activating the fight-or-flight alarm. This can result in physical sensations such as a racing heart, sweaty palms, shaking, or dizziness, and your thoughts may race.

There are times when the trigger is clear and times when it isn't. Also, a situation that may seem like a threat to one person may seem like a cakewalk to another person. And, of course, sometimes feeling anxious is correct and helpful. Not all feelings of anxiety are bad or inappropriate.

People generally feel anxiety for different reasons. When you feel anxious due to a specific stressful life situation, like giving a speech, traveling, sickness, and so on, it will often go away when the scenario ends. People with anxiety disorders, on the other hand, have chronic conditions that can severely impact their quality of life and ability to function. While several disorders can fall under this category, here are a few examples of common anxiety disorders:

Generalized anxiety disorder (GAD): A person with GAD experiences chronic worry. They worry about a number of different things, more days than not, for most of the day, and find it very difficult, if not impossible, to control their worry. The pervasive feelings of anxiety generated by the worry constantly interrupt their day, making them feel restless or on edge, irritable, and tense. The person may struggle with focusing at work, school, or home. It may cause problems with their sleep. The psychological treatment of choice for GAD is CBT, and, if necessary, medications can also be helpful.

Obsessive-compulsive disorder (OCD): People with OCD experience intrusive thoughts, images, or impulses over and over again or feel compelled to engage in rituals (mental or behavioral) that ultimately cause them great distress or disrupt their lives. For example, a person who has OCD may be excessively concerned about dirt and germs and wash their hands repeatedly due to a fear of getting themselves or others sick. Another example is the compulsion to check over and over again that the door is locked or that the stove is off due to a fear of being responsible for a break-in or a fire. The psychological treatment of choice for OCD once again is CBT, and once again medications can also be helpful.

Panic disorder (PD): People with PD experience recurrent panic attacks, often preceded by a sense of imminent dread that may seem to come out of the blue. A panic attack can make a person think they're dying, going crazy, or about to lose control. Sometimes PD can prevent a person from leaving the house because they're afraid that something dangerous will happen. This is a related condition called *agoraphobia*. Panic disorder and agoraphobia often go together, but the good news is that both are highly treatable with CBT or medication.

Social anxiety disorder (SAD): A person with SAD is fearful of being judged by other people. Social situations cause them to fear doing or saying something embarrassing. They also worry they might say or do something offensive. Those with SAD tend to avoid being around others due to their pervasive irrational fears. The condition can result in isolation and depression. Thankfully, CBT is a great treatment option for SAD. It helps people address their distorted thinking patterns and face their feared social situations so that they can ultimately be around people without experiencing anxiety and even enjoy it. (A few of the exercises in this chapter specifically address this.)

If you have an anxiety disorder or if you just want to get a handle on the anxiety you feel in certain situations, practicing CBT can help. If anxiety is interfering with your enjoyment and productivity in life, you may want to reach out to a CBT therapist for help. While anxiety can make you feel out of control or helpless, the good news is that it is highly treatable and you can take proactive steps to manage your anxious feelings. Here are a few exercises to help you understand and cope with anxiety.

VISUALIZE CALM

Imagining a place where you feel calm can help you feel less anxious. Perhaps you can visualize yourself lying on a towel on the beach or see yourself near a waterfall, in a forest, or even in your very own bedroom. Many settings can bring you to that calm state, so choose the one that works for you. This exercise is very helpful for general anxiety.

Time: 20 minutes

Format: Meditation and written exercise

Instructions: Go someplace where you can be alone, set a timer, and do the following:

1.   Lie comfortably on your bed, a yoga mat, or the floor. Close your eyes and imagine a place that brings you a sense of calm.

2.   Put one hand on your belly and breath in through your nose and out through your mouth while envisioning this calm space.

3. Feel the weight of your body on the floor or the bed, to ground yourself. (Anxiety has a way of making a person feel as if "they're out of their body," so grounding can be helpful.) You are here, right now, in this moment.

4. When the timer goes off, open your eyes. You can take that feeling of peace with you throughout the day. When you start to feel anxious, draw upon that calm place. Channel your anxious thoughts into a space of peace.

Where was your calm place? What thoughts and feelings came up during your visualization? Note if there were any cognitive distortions present and how you might reframe them.

_____

_____

_____

_____

SING OUT YOUR ANXIETY

Music is a wonderful way to express feelings. When you're anxious, there's a lot of pent-up energy. Sometimes analyzing those anxious feelings doesn't bring relief. That's where singing can help. Singing (as well as humming) is a means of distress tolerance. In other words, it's a way to tolerate the emotions within you. In addition, a funny thing happens when you sing: it can change the way thoughts feel, even though you're using

the exact same words. Thus, when you sing, you can make space for the anxiety by "defusing" it. This exercise is meant to help you express your feelings.

Time: 10 minutes

Format: Activity and written exercise

Instructions: Get in the shower and belt out your favorite song or hum the melody of your favorite tune. If you don't want to sing in the shower, do it in your car, or even walking down the street. Who cares what other people think of you? What matters most about this exercise is less thinking and more doing.

The music you choose is up to you. You might choose angry music, which some feel is a great way to express anxiety. Or maybe you'll choose an upbeat rock song to go with those anxious thoughts. Whatever you decide, use your anxious energy to communicate your frustration in song. You can even sing out your anxious thoughts! For example, you may turn your thoughts into a rap. This may help you see your thoughts as separate from who you are and make them feel less threatening. Either way, afterward, you'll likely feel more grounded and less anxious.

Which song did you choose, and how did you feel after singing it? Did your thoughts feel different when you sang them as opposed to thinking them?

_____

_____

_____

_____

START AN ANXIETY-INDUCING PROJECT

One of the things that is frustrating about anxiety is that it can be paralyzing. You want to take action, but it feels impossible. Taking one step toward starting a project can

help you feel less anxious about taking the next step, and so on.

Time: 10 minutes

Format: Written exercise and activity

Instructions: Respond to the following prompts:

1. Identify a task that feels daunting: _____

2. Break the task down into 10 small steps.

   1. _____ ☐

   2. _____ ☐

   3. _____ ☐

   4. _____ ☐

   5. _____ ☐

   6. _____ ☐

   7. _____ ☐

   8. _____ ☐

   9. _____ ☐

   10. _____ ☐

3. As you complete each step, check the box to show you completed the task.

Here is an example to help you along: Let's say you need to clean your room. You despise cleaning, and it feels unachievable. That's what anxiety wants you to believe!

You just need to do one small thing to start. Look around the floor for everything that is obviously garbage. Maybe it's old papers or wrappers from snacks. These are things that you can throw out. That's one small step to take. After that, you can identify the next step. Maybe that means taking all the clothes on the floor and putting them in the hamper.

There's no wrong way to clean a room. It's a matter of breaking the task down into smaller parts. Once you start, the more likely it is that you will finish. If you need to break a step into smaller steps, that's fine. And if you need to take breaks, that's okay, too.

Take one action toward your goal, and you will feel like you accomplished something. That feeling of accomplishment often will increase your motivation to take the next step. You'll also likely learn something important about your anxiety and your ability to manage it. You'll be surprised at the momentum created, and you will often accomplish more than you think.

TIP: While most people think that motivation comes before action, in fact, it is action (such as taking small steps as in the exercise above) that usually comes before motivation. In other words, don't wait until you feel motivated to do something, or you might wait forever! Instead, start doing something using small, manageable steps and then see how motivated you feel afterward.

EXPLORE YOUR SOCIAL ANXIETY

If you have social anxiety, you likely fear being judged or excluded in social situations. Nobody wants to be judged or excluded, so this is a normal concern. However, for some people this fear can be so magnified and paralyzing that it keeps them from seeking out and enjoying the company of others. Plus, you may then punish yourself for being afraid. The first step to combatting your social anxiety is to get to know it.

Time: 10 minutes

Format: Written exercise

Instructions: It's likely that your mind is exaggerating your fear of social situations. You are probably imagining the worst-case scenario (catastrophizing). It's crucial to

note that most of our worst fears are very unlikely to happen (fortune telling), especially socially. When you face what scares you on paper, it has less power over you.

In the following chart, list in the first column as many fears as you can think of related to social encounters. Then fill in columns two and three for each fear.

WHAT AM I AFRAID WILL HAPPEN?	WHAT'S THE LIKELIHOOD OF THAT OCCURRING?	WHAT COULD I DO IF THAT WERE TO HAPPEN?

Writing down what could potentially occur and discovering that it's not so likely to happen helps decrease the anxiety, as does realizing the outcome probably won't be as catastrophic as you believed it would be, even if it did occur. And, in the unlikely event that your feared outcome were to actually happen, you now have a plan to deal with it.

EXAMINE CORE BELIEFS TO RELIEVE SOCIAL ANXIETY

People's beliefs about themselves often have early origins in their childhood. We all form core beliefs about ourselves early in life, and they influence how we experience the world around us, as well as the rules, attitudes, and assumptions we set for ourselves. If those core beliefs are negative, we may see the world through dark-tinted glasses. In the case of social anxiety, for example, if one of your core beliefs is that you're inadequate, you might avoid people so they don't discover that you don't

measure up to others. That doesn't serve you in life. It's time to identify and challenge your core beliefs.

Time: 30 minutes

Format: Observation and written exercise

Instructions: Do an Internet search for "core beliefs" to get familiar with how they might sound. You can have both positive and negative core beliefs. Think specifically about your anxiety around social situations and see what core beliefs may be driving your desire to avoid them. Respond to the following prompts:

What is one negative core belief you've identified?

_____

_____

Where do you think it likely came from?

_____

_____

_____

What is the rule, attitude, or assumption you've set for yourself based on this belief?

_____

_____

How can you challenge and change that rule, attitude, or assumption to help you go into social situations with more confidence?

_____

_____

PRACTICE ACTIVE LISTENING IN SOCIAL SITUATIONS

When you have social anxiety or feel awkward in social settings, you may feel the need to fill the silent space in conversations. It can make you feel anxious to sit there quietly, wondering when the next person will speak. It's okay to wait and listen. Don't feel the need to jump into a conversation because you think you *should* say something. People appreciate being heard, and listening is a way to be a part of a conversation.

Time: 10 to 20 minutes

Format: Conversation and written exercise

Instructions: Ask someone you know to have a practice conversation with you. Your task is to practice active listening. Request that they talk about something they find interesting. Be mindful of what they are saying. Focus your attention outward on them, rather than inward on how you're feeling or thinking. When you want to know more, ask a question. When you don't imagine yourself to be the focus of everyone's attention, some of the social pressure is alleviated.

Even with someone you know, you may experience some negative or intrusive thoughts while you're listening to them. You might be thinking, "They think I'm weird," or "I'm so awkward." You don't have to change your thoughts. Let them be there, remind yourself that you're practicing active listening at this moment, and turn your attention back out to the speaker.

What were some of your observations about the conversation?

How much time did you spend focused on yourself? How much time did you spend focused on the other person?

_____

_____

What did you learn about the other person?

_____

_____

_____

If any cognitive distortions come up, reframe them.

_____

_____

_____

How can active listening help in social situations where you don't know the person?

_____

_____

_____

WHEN ANXIETY IS RELATED TO THE FEAR OF FAILURE

Fear of failure is a profound and overwhelming worry that happens when you envision the terrible things that could happen if you fail to achieve a goal. This often generates a great deal of anxiety, which in turn leads to procrastination or giving up. Therefore, if you want to be successful and reach your goals, you need to face your fears, despite your anxiety around them. Being anxious isn't a bad thing. In fact, it can help push you forward. Confronting your anxieties and reframing them so that you can learn to contain them and grow is powerful.

It's also essential to be *flexible* when you're working toward a goal. If your plan isn't working, you need to reevaluate your plan or revamp your strategy. Success is measured as much by how hard you work as it is by the outcome of your efforts. In addition to putting in the effort, it's crucial to examine your anxious thoughts to see if there's any evidence that they're realistic. You could be anxious about something that's extremely unlikely to occur. In some cases, there may be real obstacles in your way. In other cases, the threat is only perceived or imagined. For example, if you're worried that the book you've written isn't good and no one will like it, that's an imagined threat that needs to be challenged. On the other hand, if you plagiarized another person's words in your book and are fearful about being caught, that's a legitimate fear that needs to be resolved because it could have significant legal consequences.

Let's talk about how to differentiate between real and imagined fears so that you can feel less anxious about what's worrying you. We'll also discuss how to confront the fear of failure, work through it, and start achieving your goals.

PRACTICE POSITIVE SELF-TALK IN THE FACE OF FAILURE

This exercise allows you to confront your fears of failure, understand what negative beliefs you have about yourself in this area, and start debunking them. This technique encourages you to externalize your fears and be more objective in assessing them.

When you're more realistic, you'll likely feel less anxious—and better about yourself in general, so it's great for a self-esteem boost, too.

Time: 10 minutes

Format: Conversation (with self)

Instructions: Set up two chairs across from each other. Sit in one and face the empty seat.

Now, pretend a version of you is sitting in the empty chair. Express to that version of you all the reasons you are afraid to fail. There's nothing off-limits here. Talk about your insecurities, the worst-case scenarios, and why you're afraid to pursue this goal.

After you finish expressing your fears, switch chairs. You've heard all the negative self-talk. Now, tell yourself how it makes you feel to hear those things. If you disagree with something you said, tell that part of yourself that you don't agree and explain why.

This is also an opportunity to say positive things to the version of you who is anxious and afraid. Anything you say must be genuine. You don't have to fake being positive if you don't feel that way. Just see what comes up.

IDENTIFY YOUR WORST FEARS CONCERNING FAILURE

When you take time to write out your anxious thoughts related to your fear of failure, you start demystifying these concerns and seeing them more objectively. They may all be swirling around in your head, making them seem much more complicated and severe than they actually are. Looking at your worst fears as well as the idea of successfully undertaking a task can help you gain more control over the situation.

Time: 10 minutes

Format: Written exercise

Instructions: List everything you're afraid could happen if you try a task:

_____

_____

_____

_____

_____

_____

_____

_____

Now respond to the following prompts:

What about this project excites me? List everything good that could happen if you try.

_____

_____

_____

_____

_____

_____

_____

What three things can I do to help myself move forward?

1. _____

2. _____

3. _____

Who can I ask for help to further my project?

If something I was afraid of happening happened, what could I do to cope?

VISUALIZE YOUR SUCCESS

As children, we have vivid imaginations. Kids have dreams and can envision those coming to fruition. But as we grow older, it's harder to take our dreams seriously; many adults second-guess themselves and start telling themselves things like "That can never happen" or "I'm a failure at everything else; this will be exactly the same." By now, you probably notice the cognitive distortions in those statements. Try this visualization to see your dreams as a reality.

Time: 10 to 15 minutes

Format: Visualization and written exercise

Instructions: Go someplace where you can be alone and undisturbed. Set a timer. Sit or lie down in a comfortable position and close your eyes. Do the following:

1. Imagine that your goal for the future has been accomplished.

2. Envision where you are, what you're wearing, who is around you, and what you have done to make this dream a reality.

3. Feel the emotions associated with accomplishing your goal.

4. If thoughts of failure come up or any other negative thoughts arise, don't try to suppress them. Just let them float on by and then continue visualizing your success until the timer goes off.

5. Respond to the following prompts:

Describe your experience with the visualization:

_____

_____

_____

_____

What thoughts and feelings came up when you envisioned the successful outcome? If they were negative, how could you challenge and change them?

_____

_____

_____

_____

Remember any happy thoughts and feelings you had. Focus on those feelings when you start becoming anxious about taking steps toward your goal and the fear of failure starts to crop up. The more you practice visualizing, the better you will get at creating from your imagination. It might overwhelm or scare you to imagine success. That's something you can acknowledge, but keep moving forward and envisioning what you'd like to happen.

MANAGING ANGER

Anger is a challenging emotion for many people. Sometimes, people with impulsivity issues struggle with angry feelings. They may feel out of control when they are overcome with anger and say or do something hurtful that they later regret. Often, anger comes if we perceive an injustice has occurred without checking the facts or examining the usefulness of our personal rules for justice. CBT is a wonderful tool that you can use to gain more awareness of your anger cues and examine your rules. CBT will help you be more flexible in situations so that you can better manage your anger.

Keep in mind that, like anxiety, anger is a normal human emotion. But when anger gets out of control, it may impact not only your relationships but also your physical health. Research published in the *Journal of Interpersonal Violence* and the *Journal of Psychosomatic Research*, among others, shows that people who get angry often and don't manage their anger can have weaker immune systems. Others develop high blood pressure or heart disease. For all these reasons, it's crucial to learn to manage your anger. The first step comes with awareness. What's making you angry? What are your triggers? How do you experience anger? Where in your body do you feel it? How can you learn to calm your mind and body when you feel angry?

Keep in mind that anger is a normal human emotion, and not all anger is bad. Sometimes anger is entirely valid. Justifiable anger is when you are angry with a cause. Sometimes things in life happen and there's a clear reason to be outraged. What matters is what you *do* with that anger. One of the most frustrating things is wanting to take action but feeling paralyzed. Over time, that could result in an explosive rage, because the anger is pent-up. People who have difficulty with anger management might react in an extreme manner when they're upset. Their anger may seem justified, but their explosive response is not. Anger, even when justifiable, is typically influenced by cognitive distortions. Here are some examples of sources of justifiable anger:

Trauma. A person who experienced a traumatic event may experience feelings of anger or rage. It's understandable that they will have these emotions, as people with a trauma history often reexperience their trauma in the here and now. It's important for this individual to work through their feelings on their own and, if necessary, with a trauma therapist.

When a criminal isn't punished for their actions. If someone committed a heinous crime, such as murder, rape, or kidnapping, and the law doesn't punish them, that may cause the victim (or the public) to be angry. Lower intensity versions of this may be

when we see someone else getting away with something—like speeding, falsely calling out sick from work, or breaking some other rule.

Your child is mistreated in school. Parents get angry when their children are bullied in a school environment or seem to be treated unfairly by teachers or other authority figures. Anger in all these situations is understandable.

Remember, it's okay—and even adaptive—to feel angry from time to time. Like anxiety, anger can motivate you into action. However, it's what you do with the anger that matters, as actions can be productive or destructive, depending on how you channel your anger. Let's take the third example: A parent is angry because their child is being bullied. If that person walks into the school and punches the child or the teacher in the face, even though their anger may feel justified, this isn't productive. Their action physically harmed a person and will likely have negative consequences for everyone involved. Instead of resorting to physical violence, the parent could call a meeting with the administration to talk about the bullying. If that doesn't work and the situation escalates, the parent can present their case to the school district. There are many productive actions a person can take that don't involve harming others.

Whether anger is valid or not, there are four ways people who feel angry can choose to communicate it: open aggression, passive aggression, passivity, and assertiveness. Let's take a look at each with some examples before we move on to the exercises.

Open Aggression

Open aggression is the easiest to spot because it is direct. At best, however, it is often perceived by others as disrespectful, and it can also tip into displays of rage, such as when people bottle up their anger to the point where it becomes explosive. That's a more intense form of open aggression. Those who struggle with open aggression may engage in destructive behaviors where they verbally or physically hurt themselves and others. They can be intimidating, intentionally or unintentionally. An openly aggressive person may be seen as a bully. This person could engage in physical fights, break things out of anger, or abuse others. This sort of anger can damage relationships, sometimes to the point where they're irreparable. There are books and courses that can help you or your loved ones cope with these emotions. The bottom line is that when anger is out of control, it can be dangerous and it needs attention.

Here's an example of open aggression: You're in the movie theater and a person behind you is kicking the back of your chair. You spin around and threaten to break the person's legs if they don't knock it off.

Passive Aggression

It can be difficult for some people to express anger. It's an uncomfortable emotion for some. Their solution is to express their angry feelings in passive-aggressive ways, which still allow them to let others know they're angry, but indirectly. For example, a person may give a backhanded compliment. If you're taking a long time to dress for a party, and your friend is angry but they don't know how to express it directly, they could make a passive-aggressive jab such as, "I'm glad you took so much time to put on your makeup, you look perfect, it really hides your flaws." It's sarcastic, and it's not a compliment. Another popular example of a passive-aggressive remark is when someone asks you what's wrong, and you say, "I'm fine," but sigh audibly as if things are not okay and mutter, "What do you care, anyway?" People typically engage in this behavior because anger makes them uncomfortable and they don't know how to express it in a healthy manner.

Here's an example of passive aggression: You're in the movie theater and a person behind you is kicking the back of your chair. You don't confront the chair kicker but make very loud comments about how rude people are these days, or you try to sit up taller in your seat to block the chair kicker's view in retaliation.

Passivity

In his excellent self-help book *The Assertiveness Workbook: How to Express Your Ideas and Stand Up for Yourself at Work and in Relationships*, Dr. Randy Paterson outlines different forms of communication. Just because you are passive doesn't mean you're not angry. In fact, you may want to communicate your anger but struggle to come up with the best way to do so. The benefit here is that you come across as people-pleasing or accommodating. However, on the inside, you often find yourself furious and can't seem to express how you feel. Maybe you're worried about how your emotions will impact others. You could be fearful of rejection. Whatever the reasons behind your passivity, it's crucial to explore them. Being passive is an unhealthy way to deal with anger. It can result in strained relationships. Instead of internalizing your anger, it's best to learn ways to express it.

Here's an example of passivity: You're in the movie theater and a person behind you is kicking the back of your chair. You just sit there, upset and angry, unable to enjoy or focus on the movie but unwilling to do anything about the situation. Instead, you wonder why fate always seems to put you in these predicaments.

Assertiveness

Assertiveness is the healthiest way of expressing anger. You've learned the triggers that make you angry and can express your anger with respect for both the person it's directed at and yourself. You don't internalize it or hold it in to the point where it gets out of control.

You can learn to be assertive in your communication style. Remember that sometimes anger is justified. In fact, recognizing when anger is justified can be adaptive. Anger is often a sign that you sense some injustice may be occurring and that something needs to be done to amend the situation. Assertiveness starts with you expressing your feelings. The steps to doing this are to identify what's making you angry and why it's making you angry, and then get the anger out. That could mean confronting the person or people you think did something wrong. Maybe you need to write down your feelings to get clarity on why you feel angry. You might need to take a walk or run or do some exercise to regulate your anger.

Here's an example of assertiveness: You're in the movie theater and a person behind you is kicking the back of your chair. You turn around calmly, look the chair kicker in eye while calmly but firmly pointing out that having your chair kicked is distracting, and tell them to stop.

In the following exercises, we'll show you how to practice assertiveness, get your feelings out, and feel heard. We'll also explore productive ways to manage anger. When something happens to trigger your anger, it's important to examine both the trigger and your reaction to it to assess whether your thoughts are accurate and to figure out how to cope with it so neither you nor other people are left feeling disrespected.

SPELL OUT THE ANGER

Instead of immediately expressing the anger, think about why you're angry and write it down. Sometimes it helps to spell it out. You can write stream of consciousness thoughts, which don't need to sound cohesive. The most important thing here is to simply express the anger in the written word.

Time: 20 minutes

Format: Written exercise

Instructions: Respond to the following prompts to spell out the anger:

What was the trigger that made you feel angry?

_____

_____

Who was involved?

_____

_____

Why are you angry? What rule for living did you think was being broken?

_____

_____

_____

What, if any, cognitive distortions do you recognize in your thoughts? How can you reframe them?

_____

_____

_____

What action do you want to take to deal with the anger?

_____

_____

_____

If you could say anything to the person or people who triggered your anger, what would you say?

_____

_____

_____

Once you know the source of the anger, you can figure out what to do about it, if anything. That could mean talking to the person or people who made you mad. That's when practicing assertive communication can help.

COMMUNICATE ANGER ASSERTIVELY

After writing about your anger and reframing any cognitive distortions, you can practice communicating your anger assertively to the person you are angry with. You're prepared with the information about what made you angry and have the words to express it. You can refer to what you wrote in the previous exercise if needed. That might sound strange, but that's the place where you have the information you want to share. Because expressing anger can be challenging, it helps to have your emotions documented in one place.

Time: 15 minutes

Format: Conversation

Instructions: Let the person know that you want to have a conversation about what made you angry. Remember to use "I" statements (see page 68) to help you focus on your feelings rather than blaming the other person. The other person will then be more likely to be receptive to your feelings, and their reply may be more empathetic and understanding.

The DEARMAN technique used in dialectical behavior therapy (DBT), which is another version of CBT, is an excellent way to communicate your feelings in a clear way. DEARMAN stands for:

Describe the situation and stick to the facts. Don't get emotional. Just paint a picture of what happened.

Express how you feel about the situation.

Assert yourself.

Reinforce your request.

Mindfulness is crucial.

Appear confident.

Negotiate.

As you talk to the other person about the situation that made you angry, keep DEARMAN in mind. Remember to listen to their point of view as well.

BREATHE OUT ANGER, BREATHE IN CALM

You may have heard the expression "seeing red." When people feel angry, their focus narrows. Their attention gets directed toward what they believe is the source of their anger. That's the red involved here. In this exercise, you will use color meditation to release feelings of anger.

Time: 10 minutes

Format: Visualization and breathing exercise

Instructions: Imagine you are a mystical and powerful dragon that breathes out fire when you're angry. Close your eyes and visualize yourself as this dragon. Take a breath and breathe out the red fire of anger. Notice where the red anger sits in your body.

As you breathe in, imagine breathing in a calming white light. As you breathe out, tell yourself that it's okay to let go of the anger. Letting go doesn't mean you don't have a right to feel angry. You're simply allowing your body to regain some calmness so

you can observe the situation in a more balanced, regulated way, and likely see more choices in how you can respond. Repeat for about 10 minutes.

After you breathe through the angry feelings, they should feel less intense and more manageable, and you should then be able to make a productive strategy to deal with the issue that's causing your anger.

TIME THE ANGER

Sometimes when you feel angry, it seems like it won't ever diminish or end. You imagine feeling angry forever. That's often what makes a person want to act on their anger right away. You're eager to let your feelings out so that you don't have to feel them anymore. That's why putting anger into the context of a time frame can help.

Time: 10 minutes

Format: Observation

Instructions: Observe your feelings of anger over time. Test out how long you think it is going to last versus how long it actually lasts—or, at least, stays so intense. Try to just observe your feelings and the sensations in your body. Don't try to do anything with them. Just "surf" them, like a surfer does a wave in the ocean.

You can also ask yourself, "Will I still be angry about this in a week? Is this something I will still be angry about next year?" Often, this is not likely to be the case. However, if you feel that your anger will be long-lasting, you may want to look for cognitive distortions. If that doesn't help or if you constantly find yourself feeling angry, you may want to explore this with a therapist.

Stripping Away Anger, Brick by Brick

The trouble with anger is it can build up over time. That's why it's crucial to find healthy ways to express it. Bottling up anger can lead to aggressive outbursts. It's like a teakettle that's bubbling at a boil and then all of a sudden starts to whistle. That's how anger can be. If you learn to regularly express yourself assertively, it can help you process the anger, you'll be less likely to be overwhelmed by it, and you'll be more effective at expressing it.

Some people feel overwhelmed when they experience anger because they fear that they will lash out or do something that will hurt someone. This is all the more reason to learn anger management exercises so that you can find ways to express yourself more assertively and prevent the anger from building up. You don't have to feel out of control just because you're angry. Here are some more techniques to help you manage anger.

REFRAME ANGER AS IF AN OUTSIDER

In this exercise, you will bring up a memory of a time you were angry and practice reframing it from an outside point of view. The point of this exercise is not to get angry all over again but to examine the anger from a more objective standpoint. The goal is to find alternative ways to deal with anger in the future, rather than acting impulsively or letting anger get the best of you.

Time: 15 minutes

Format: Visualization and written exercise

Instructions: Find a comfortable seat where you can be alone, and then do the following:

1. Close your eyes for 15 seconds and imagine a time you were angry.

2. Write down what was going on in that moment:

_____

_____

_____

_____

3. Now that you have the situation in your mind, close your eyes again and recall the memory where you were angry, but imagine you are an outside observer. Look at yourself from a third-person perspective.

4. Notice how you were standing and where the other person was. What did your face look like? How did the other person appear?

5. What do you notice from the outside, as opposed to looking at the situation from your perspective?

6. Now open your eyes and write down the difference in feelings. Did you feel a certain way when you remembered the situation? Was your experience looking at your situation as an outside observer different?

7. Close your eyes once more and imagine the situation again from the perspective of an outside observer, this time focusing on what you could have done differently instead of getting mad.

Describe your angry memory again in the space provided, this time incorporating what you learned by taking a new perspective. If you notice any remaining cognitive distortions, see if you can reframe them.

EXTERNALIZE ANGER

It doesn't help to think about yourself as an "angry person." Anger is an emotion. While anger is something you experience internally, it can be helpful to see it as something outside yourself. If the anger inside you were to take a physical form, think about how it would look. Maybe the anger appears as a tornado or broken glass. Perhaps the anger is a red monster that flies around, trying to hurt you. There's no wrong answer to how anger might appear to you.

Time: 15 minutes

Format: Drawing activity and written exercise

Instructions: In the space provided, draw the anger. This helps you externalize the anger so it's not conflated with your identity. When you can imagine it as separate from you, it's easier to find ways to distance yourself from it and be in a better place to work with your feelings.

The crucial component of this exercise is to view the anger as separate from your identity. It's not you. It's "your anger." Feelings are generated by thoughts, even if they are about the past or future, and even if they are not based in reality. When you develop the skill of identifying your feelings and managing them, they can serve as useful messages and can help you process what's happening in your life.

Now take a look at the anger you drew. Describe it. What does it look like? How do you feel toward it? Is there anything underneath the anger? Ask it what it needs from you. You are interacting with an external force and learning to better understand what the anger is and how to be accepting of it and compassionate toward it. If any cognitive distortions come up for you, try to reframe them.

LESSONS LEARNED

We all need to cope with stress, anxiety, and anger. They are normal responses to the unpleasant things that happen in life. Whether the triggers are constant or occasional, you've been practicing skills that can help you cope with each emotion. Meditation, observation, reframing, externalization, and other activities can help you find calm and clarity around otherwise negative thoughts, feelings, and situations. Flip back through this chapter and review your entries. Think about the experiences you had with each exercise. Respond to the following prompts:

Which exercise was most helpful and why?

_____

_____

_____

Which exercise was your least favorite? Do you need to give it another try?

_____

_____

_____

Did you skip any exercises? Why?

_____

_____

What is the most valuable lesson you learned from this chapter?

_____

_____

_____

_____

What do you still need to work on?

_____

_____

_____

_____

What is the next action you will take and when will you take it?

_____

_____

_____

_____

5

LETTING GO OF GUILT AND SHAME

Guilt has to do with an action you have or haven't taken that you believe is bad or wrong and you accept responsibility for. Guilt causes us to focus our attention on the feelings of others. On the other hand, CBT typically views shame as something that results from believing we have violated a social norm. Shame makes us direct our focus inward and view our entire self in a negative light. These ideas are usually related to concepts that suggest we are flawed, inadequate, bad, or wrong in some way. In both cases, practicing CBT can help you resolve these uncomfortable emotions and lessen their impact on you in the future. Let's dig in so you have the tools to dig yourself out.

5

A LOOK AT GUILT

Guilt is an emotion that comes up when you believe you have done something wrong. Often, it's accompanied by a related thought that you could have or should have done better or that you should not have done something at all. There's guilt we generate for ourselves and guilt generated by the words or behaviors of others. Guilt is also usually discussed in terms of "helpful" or "unhelpful." Sometimes guilt is a cue that we have violated our own standards or norms and something needs to be repaired. Sometimes guilt is unhelpful because it stems from unrealistic expectations we have for ourselves or others have for us.

Excessive guilt can feel overwhelming and distracting, leading to thoughts of hopelessness and helplessness. People who often feel guilty are usually stuck in self-deprecation mode. They ruminate over what they did "wrong" and often worry they may have offended someone. They may even feel like a "bad" or immoral person. If this describes you, the guilt you feel is likely tied to certain thoughts as well as you not knowing what actions to take to remedy the situation. You'll learn some helpful strategies soon.

Feeling Guilt Isn't Empathy

Empathy is the ability to understand and share the feelings of another person. If one of your loved ones is suffering, you likely empathize with their struggles. However, if you're prone to often feeling guilty, you might also wonder if you did something to contribute to that person's pain or if you failed to help them in some way. It's normal to feel empathy when someone you love is struggling with something; you want to under-stand their pain and make it better if you can. However, guilt is different from empathy. When you feel guilty, you are blaming yourself for their pain. On the other hand, if you think you caused their pain through your actions and they say that this is the case and their assessment rings true to you, then guilt is a valid response and you can go about correcting it.

When We Strive to Avoid Guilt

Because guilt is a painful emotion, it's natural to not want to feel guilty. Some people are so uncomfortable with the feeling that they blame others rather than take account-ability for their own actions. It's often easier to point the finger at another person than it is to take responsibility. Some people try to circumvent feeling guilty by excessively

asking for reassurance or forgiveness. If this describes you, instead of blaming others for how you feel, learn to own up to your mistakes and take the appropriate actions to remedy them. Feeling guilty for something you've done without taking action doesn't accomplish anything, and blaming others for your uncomfortable feelings will likely only make things worse.

Guilt Associated with Overindulgence

Overindulgence in food, alcohol, drugs, shopping, and so on, is a common trap that many people fall into. We'll talk more about this in chapter 6 when we discuss cravings, but let's look at it from this "guilt" angle first. When people overindulge, for whatever reason, they tend to feel guilty afterward (which, ironically, then makes them even more likely to overindulge). Here are three common reasons people might overindulge:

Emotion regulation: To cope with strong negative emotions. The feelings are too difficult to face, so you try to manage them by indulging in something you enjoy, even if it comes with a cost. Let's say you eat a box of cookies because you feel anxious. You no longer feel anxious, for the time being, but you now feel guilty for having eaten a whole box of cookies. Many things can fall into this category, not just food.

Brain chemicals: When you engage in something you enjoy, your brain releases dopamine, a neurotransmitter that makes you feel good. You may want to keep that "happy hormone" going, so you continue the behavior to excess and wind up overindulging on whatever it is.

Peer pressure: When you're around friends or family who are drinking and eating at a party, for instance, they might pressure you to have a drink or try another dessert. Maybe you planned to have a single drink, but before you know it, you keep filling your wineglass, or maybe you wind up eating so much food that you feel ready to explode. While this type of subtle pressure can be challenging to resist, it's a slippery slope toward overindulgence and the guilty feelings that result from it.

No matter the reason for your overindulgence, it's crucial to figure out what seems to help and what seems to make it worse. This can be accomplished with awareness training. You can work on that awareness by journaling, monitoring your behaviors, confiding in a friend, or even talking about it with a therapist. Here is an exercise you can do to become more aware of your patterns of overindulgence so that you can wake up the next day without those guilty feelings.

CONFRONT OVERINDULGENCE WITH THE ABC MODEL

Guilt is often a consequence of overindulgence, but it can go deeper. You likely feel guilty because whatever you have indulged in has some greater consequences that negatively impact you in some way. Become aware of what seems to trigger your tendency to overindulge and the consequences of it so that you can learn from past guilt. You can do this with the ABC model. ABC stands for "antecedent, belief, and consequence." In this instance, you will address the overindulgent behavior that causes you to feel guilt, but this model works for any behavior you want to change.

Time: 10 minutes

Format: Written exercise

Instructions: Examine the triggers (the antecedent) behind the behavior you want to change, as well as the belief that led to the emotional and behavioral consequences. Using the chart provided, respond to the following prompts:

1. In the row labeled "Antecedent," write down anything that appears to have triggered the problematic behavior and feelings of guilt. For example, let's say you had a fight with your significant other.

2. In the row labeled "Belief," note the negative thoughts you had in the moment. Perhaps you thought, "They don't love me! This relationship is over!"

3. In the row labeled "Consequences," write down what you did (behavioral consequence) and how you felt (emotional consequence) as a result. Label each as positive or negative. Perhaps you called them a name, hung up on them, and then went out drinking and now feel guilty for what you said to them and the fact that you overindulged in alcohol.

ANTECEDENT	

BELIEF	
CONSEQUENCES (EMOTIONAL AND BEHAVORIAL)	

TIP: Another important part of changing your behavior is to be mindful of how everyday events impact your thinking. Awareness is the first step toward healing. You can also use the ABC model to note any beliefs that cause you to think negatively about yourself. Were there negative thoughts that went through your mind? Did you notice any cognitive distortions? These can also lead to guilty feelings, so be mindful when you're noting them.

Dealing with Guilt Trips

Guilt-tripping is a form of manipulation used by people in an attempt to make others feel bad. Sometimes people engage in the behavior to feel superior to others; other times, they want a sense of control over other people. If someone is guilt-tripping you, they might sense that you are going against what they want you to do, so rather than engage you in a productive, assertive conversation about it, they try to get you to fall in line with their wants or desires. This person may also try to make you feel bad for asserting yourself.

If you recognize in hindsight that you've been guilt-tripped by someone, you might feel resentful and duped. You might wonder, "How could someone I care about do this to me?" Sometimes people don't realize that they're guilt-tripping you, so an assertive conversation might be necessary. However, if you sense that the guilt-tripping is intentional, there are ways to combat it.

COMBAT GUILT TRIPS BY IDENTIFYING COGNITIVE DISTORTIONS

There are times when we are on the receiving end of a guilt trip and struggle with the feelings it brings up in us, and we need help in assessing if something really is our fault. Identifying the cognitive distortions in the triggered thoughts and feelings can help you sort out fact from fiction so you can take action (if you feel the situation calls for it) on only the facts.

Time: 10 minutes

Format: Written exercise

Instructions: Use the chart provided to fill in each category listed in the left column. What thought are you having as a result of a guilt trip? List it in the first row. What feelings does this thought bring up? Enter those in the second row. What cognitive distortions are at work here? Write them in the third row. How can you reframe the thought to be more helpful? Jot that down in the fourth row. If you are having difficulty, see the example after the chart.

THOUGHT	
FEELING(S)	
COGNITIVE DISTORTION(S)	
REFRAME	

Here's an example: Your friend wants you to watch their pet for a week while they go on vacation. You'd really like to help out, but you just don't have the time and energy, so you can't commit to doing it. The friend then tries to guilt-trip you by reminding you of all the times they were there to help you out, stressing how easy it would be to do it, and emphasizing how they have no one else to do it and may have to cancel their vacation if you don't say yes.

At this point, you have the right to take a pause from the conversation and work through your feelings, whether this conversation is in person, on the phone, or by text. You can tell your friend you're sorry they are upset, but you need a break to process your feelings.

Your automatic **thought** might be, "I am a bad friend for not helping them out." This may lead to **feelings** of guilt because you believe that "a good friend would do it." This is an example of the labeling **cognitive distortion**. You called yourself a "bad friend." You may also believe that this person will be so upset with you that they will no longer want to be your friend. There are multiple cognitive distortions at work here, including *jumping to conclusions* (mind reading and fortune telling) and *magnification* (catastrophizing). You don't know what your friend believes unless you ask them, and you don't know that this conflict will spell the end of your friendship forever.

In the fourth row, you could **reframe** the thought by saying, "I'm not a bad friend for not helping them out. There are lots of ways in which I am good friend to them. It's unfortunate that I can't be there for them this time, but I would not want to commit to taking care of a pet when I know my schedule won't allow it. We've been upset with each other before and managed to work through it. Our friendship is strong enough to make it through this conflict."

By reframing your thoughts, you can diminish guilty feelings and discover new ways to gain clarity on the reality of the situation, which will lead to a more productive way to deal with similar situations in the future.

WORK OUT GUILT DUE TO MISCOMMUNICATION

Miscommunications and misunderstandings can sometimes cause you to feel guilty for your actions or nonactions. This is a guilt trip you put on yourself. It's a bad feeling, but there's something you can do about it: you can apologize to the other person for your

part in the communication disconnection. People make mistakes, and you can rectify yours by atoning for your actions, which may help alleviate your guilt.

Time: 10 minutes

Format: Written exercise

Instructions: Think about a situation where you misunderstood what someone wanted or needed you to do. Here's an example: Let's say you and your friend had plans to see a movie, and they bought tickets in advance. You mixed up the time of the film. The show was at 5 p.m., but you thought it was at 8 p.m. You had a long day at work, so you took a nap to rest up for the evening out. You missed your friend's calls and texts, and they were waiting at the theater. You feel guilty because you inconvenienced your friend. There's no need to berate yourself for being a bad friend; it's just a bad feeling. You can apologize and reimburse them for the ticket.

Using your real-life example, explore what happened here:

Situation: _____

_____

_____

_____

My actions: _____

_____

_____

_____

Their actions: _____

_____

_____

_____

Miscommunication: _____

_____

_____

_____

Result: _____

_____

_____

_____

Feeling: _____

_____

_____

_____

What can I do to solve the problem? _____

_____

_____

CREATE BOUNDARY AFFIRMATIONS AROUND GUILT

When you're constantly being guilt-tripped by someone, you can end up feeling powerless in the relationship. However, there are boundaries you can set to protect yourself. Before you speak to a person who is trying to manipulate your emotions by guilt-tripping you, state an affirmation that makes you feel strong and reinforces your boundaries.

Time: 15 to 20 minutes

Format: Written exercise and conversation

Instructions: An affirmation can remind you to stay true to your wants and desires and prevent you from being manipulated. Here are a few examples of affirmations you may want to use, or you can create your own:

→ I am not responsible for other people's feelings.

→ My emotions count, and so do my needs.

→ I can validate another person's feelings without sacrificing what I need.

→ My opinion matters as much as other people's opinions.

Write your affirmation here:

Who is guilt-tripping you, and how can this affirmation help you avoid feeling unnecessarily guilty?

Before your next conversation with this person, repeat your affirmation to yourself several times. If you feel comfortable, you can say your affirmation out loud during the conversation with the other person.

Guilt in Families

Family members can make a deep impact on you with their words. If you have a profound and emotionally charged history with your family, it's likely you're carrying around some guilt. Close family members know you inside and out, including your strengths and vulnerabilities. You may feel helpless and beholden to your family, as if you must do or be what they're asking of you. If you aren't what they expect or don't do what they want, feeling guilty is a likely consequence.

Even though you are part of a family unit, it's crucial to maintain a sense of self. Just because they are your family doesn't mean you must be who they want you to be or do what they want you to do. Their wants, needs, and behavior are about them, not you. The following exercises promote self-awareness and grounding so that you can feel more confident when dealing with your family and assuaging guilt.

INCREASE YOUR COPING SKILLS

It's essential to have a toolbox of coping skills to manage your emotions so that you can stay grounded when a family member makes a request of you that becomes emotionally charged when you say no.

Time: 15 minutes

Format: Written exercise

Instructions: After a conversation with a family member leads you to feel guilty for something you've done, haven't done, or won't do, choose among the following techniques and then respond to the prompts:

Distraction: Guilty feelings can be painful or trigger anger. Acknowledge these emotions, but don't let them rule your day. It's okay to distract yourself and take a break. Take a walk, call a friend, play a game on your phone, or watch a show. It will help reset your mood.

Sit with your feelings: You're distressed, and that's okay. Your emotions are real, and it's okay to experience your feelings. Sometimes it feels like the intensity of the emotion won't end, but it will. And after that, you can move forward with more confidence, knowing you can handle that intense emotion.

Breathe: Before reacting, take some relaxing deep breaths. You would be surprised at how much better you can feel after breathing. Your breath is one thing you have control over, and it has the potential to change your entire physiological and emotional state.

Respond to the following prompts:

Who were you talking to when feelings of guilt came up? Describe the scenario.

_____

_____

_____

What thoughts came up that were associated with the feelings of guilt?

_____

_____

_____

Which technique did you use? How effective was it and why?

_____

_____

_____

Which technique might you try next time? Can you think of another coping skill that might help?

_____

_____

_____

$$\boxed{\text{TRY EMPATHY}}$$

You know your family better than anyone. You also understand *their* triggers, what helps them, and what doesn't help them. Instead of focusing on how your family member is making *you* feel, try to empathize with them. There might be something going on that's causing them to try to make you feel guilty. Perhaps they're feeling pain and are trying to deflect it onto you.

Time: 15 minutes

Format: Conversation and written exercise

Instructions: When feeling guilty is a consequence of asserting yourself with a family member, you might have all kinds of negative emotions toward that person. Even though what they're saying makes you uncomfortable, try to redirect the focus to them and empathize with what they're feeling.

During your next conversation, ask questions like "What's going on?" "How are you feeling right now?" and "Are you okay?" You genuinely want to know what's happening with them and show them that you care.

Rather than take things personally, consider the idea that it may be more about them than you. Doing so will empower you, could make them feel better, and could potentially get to the source of why they are giving you such a hard time that you come away from the conversation feeling guilty.

On the following page, brainstorm how you might empathize with your family member about a situation that has come up in the past.

_____

_____

_____

_____

TAKE PERSONAL RESPONSIBILITY

If a family member is upset with you about something and you feel guilty as a result, taking time to understand your responsibility in this situation will help you clarify what actions, if any, you need to take.

Time: 10 minutes

Format: Written exercise

Instructions: Respond to the following prompts to determine your role in the situation:

What is my family member saying that is causing me to feel guilty? Is it based on fact or opinion?

_____

_____

_____

What other emotions am I experiencing?

_____

_____

_____

What is my responsibility in this situation?

_____

_____

What action, if any, do I need to take?

_____

_____

Here's an example: Your sister says, "If you're not at the party, it just won't be the same. I _really_ want you to be there, and I'll be sad if you're not. I won't be able to enjoy myself. Can't you just tell your boss that you can't be on call that night? What if you have to go into work at the last minute?"

That the party won't be the same without you is your sister's opinion. Yes, she'll be sad if you're not there, and she's entitled to those feelings, just as you're entitled to yours. You may feel guilty for possibly letting her down, sad you might miss the party, and maybe resentful that she wants you to tell your boss you can't be on call even though it could interfere with an upcoming promotion opportunity.

Your responsibility is simply to do your best to attend, but you may not be able to go if you get called into work, and that's okay, too. You are not responsible for her enjoyment at the party. Your sister is responsible for her own enjoyment, even if you're not there. The reality is that you can only do your best, and that's good enough. If it helps to assert that sentiment, do so: "I'll do the best I can."

When Guilt Turns to Self-Loathing

Guilt and self-loathing are connected. Let's say you feel guilty because you accidentally spoiled a surprise party by telling your friend it was going to happen. You can't stop thinking about the mistake, and negative thoughts come up. You think, "I always ruin everything." You can't seem to stop the cognitive distortions from surfacing. You start to believe that you're a bad person, which leads to thoughts of self-loathing.

It's crucial to understand the warning signs of self-loathing so you can understand how to cope with these issues. You may be engaging in self-loathing if you're having defeatist thoughts such as, "There's no point in trying; I'm a failure anyway," or "I'm

incompetent. I can't do anything right." You could be self-loathing when you're physically neglecting yourself. You stop engaging in self-care, such as bathing or eating well. A person who dislikes themselves may isolate from others, causing them to feel depressed and further reinforcing the idea that people don't want to be around them. If you're experiencing these symptoms, it's crucial to reach out to a mental health professional to get guidance on how to start caring for yourself.

To break the cycle of self-loathing, you'll need to figure out your triggers. Ask yourself, "What are my insecurities?" (See Keep a Negative Thought Log on page 136 for more on this.) Self-loathing may also come from past traumatic experiences. Maybe you were raised in a household where your parents were hypercritical of your behavior. That type of parenting could leave a person thinking that no matter what they do, it's not good enough and there's something wrong with them. Other factors might contribute to a sense of self-loathing, but no matter the cause, you can practice some exercises to work through difficult emotions. And if you're still struggling after using this book, perhaps it's a good idea to speak to a therapist to help you work through this issue.

REFRAME SELF-LOATHING TO SELF-COMPASSION

When you are beset by self-loathing thoughts, show yourself some compassion. This might feel difficult when you're used to having self-deprecating thoughts, but the more you practice self-compassion, the more natural it will feel. When you are compassionate with yourself, it can relieve some of the negative feelings you have about yourself.

Time: 10 to 15 minutes

Format: Written exercise

Instructions: In the following chart, record your self-loathing thoughts in the first column. For example, they could be automatic thoughts like "I'm bad at keeping promises" or "I'm a terrible friend." In the second column, respond to each self-loathing thought with a compassionate response. One way to reply to "I'm a terrible friend" would be: "It sounds like you're feeling pressure to be a good friend. I can see why you're hurting."

SELF-LOATHING THOUGHT	COMPASSIONATE RESPONSE

KEEP A NEGATIVE THOUGHT LOG

Keeping a record of your self-loathing thoughts can help you identify whether there are any common themes among them. Once you are aware of what these common thoughts are, you can start to examine them and see if these beliefs about yourself have any validity. When you see them written out in your thought log, you can view them more objectively and challenge them to see which cognitive distortions are in play.

Time: 10 to 15 minutes

Format: Written exercise

Instructions: Use the following chart to record any repetitive negative thoughts or ideas that pop up for you.

DATE: _____

NEGATIVE THOUGHT: _____

FEELING: _____

COGNITIVE DISTORTION(S): _____

REFRAME: _____

DATE: _____

NEGATIVE THOUGHT: _____

FEELING: _____

COGNITIVE DISTORTION(S): _____

REFRAME: _____

DATE: _____

NEGATIVE THOUGHT: _____

FEELING: _____

COGNITIVE DISTORTION(S): _____

REFRAME: _____

DATE: _____

NEGATIVE THOUGHT: _____

FEELING: _____

COGNITIVE DISTORTION(S): _____

REFRAME: _____

DATE: _____

NEGATIVE THOUGHT: _____

FEELING: _____

COGNITIVE DISTORTION(S): _____

REFRAME: _____

DATE: _____

NEGATIVE THOUGHT: _____

FEELING: _____

COGNITIVE DISTORTION(S): _____

REFRAME: _____

DATE: _____

NEGATIVE THOUGHT: _____

FEELING: _____

COGNITIVE DISTORTION(S): _____

REFRAME: _____

Not sure where to start? Let's say you feel like you "talk too much" when you meet new people and you can't stand that you do this. Perhaps you feel guilty later for not letting other people talk about themselves, and you berate yourself for being a "bad listener" or coming across as "too self-important." Perhaps your negative thought is "No one likes me." This is a self-loathing thought that you can start to work on once you are aware of it.

After a week, take a look at your log to see if there are themes you need to analyze. It's not crucial to investigate the origins of these ideas, but it may help you to understand them better, put them into context, and distance yourself from them.

ACKNOWLEDGE YOUR STRENGTHS

When you're used to self-loathing thoughts circulating in your mind and you feel guilty for "being such a failure," it's easy to lose sight of what you're good at and what you have to be proud of. Taking note of your strengths and skills can help you put your focus on a goal that, once accomplished, you can feel good about. Participating in an activity you enjoy and know you do well can help decrease those feelings of self-loathing.

Time: 15 to 30 minutes

Format: Written exercise and activity

Instructions: In the space provided, list your strengths and skills. Your list doesn't need to be extensive. It could be three to five items that you know you're good at.
   My strengths and skills are:

1. _____

2. _____

3. _____

4. _____

5. _____

   Read this list back to yourself and think of one activity you can engage in that requires one of your strengths or skills. For example, if you're good at baking, choose a recipe to make, shop for the ingredients, and then bake away. Whatever it is, go do it. Can't think of any? Ask someone you know and trust to help! Still struggling to find some? Use it as a challenge to start building some strengths and skills in areas that are important to you. Just be sure to take small steps!

A LOOK AT SHAME

As mentioned, CBT typically views shame as something that results from believing we have violated a social norm. Shame makes us direct our focus inward and view our entire self in a negative light. These thoughts are usually that we are flawed, inadequate, bad, or wrong in some way. Shame is painful to hold on to and can weigh you down. Shame is often linked to experiencing a social threat, which makes a person feel anxious or scared. When threatened, the adrenal gland is stimulated and releases cortisol, a stress hormone. That can result in a racing heart, sweating, and other fight-flight-freeze symptoms. Your muscles may tense up and you may have trouble concentrating.

Imagine you have a public speaking engagement and you make a joke that offends a group of people in the audience. A reporter writes a disparaging article about your speech and says some cruel things about your character. It's natural that you would have feelings of shame about the event. You could internally punish yourself. With guilt, one might respond to this experience with the thought "I wish I hadn't done that" and the behavior that would attempt to repair the situation. But a shame response would involve the thought "I am a terrible person," along with efforts to hide or conceal the action from yourself and others, all while you were feeling those uncomfortable physical symptoms.

Clinical psychologist Dr. Albert Ellis, another early pioneer in the field of CBT and the founder of rational emotive behavior therapy (REBT), focused on how people could challenge irrational beliefs about themselves and the world to deal with emotional hurdles, one of which is shame. Dr. Ellis emphasized how people have both rational and irrational patterns of thinking, which is basically what you've been working on throughout this workbook (and was featured in the "ABC model" for overindulgence exercise earlier in this chapter). When a person thinks rationally, they are productive and help themselves. When a person thinks irrationally, it is often linked to problematic emotions, as well as maladaptive or even destructive actions. In other words, Ellis believed that people create emotional challenges for themselves based on how they think (i.e., other people can't upset us; rather, we upset ourselves over how we think about what other people do or say). Therefore, when you experience shame, it's a result of your belief (potentially irrational) that you've violated some moral code. It helps to know this so that you can challenge your beliefs around shame. The exercises that follow will help you do that.

Express Your Shame

It can help to talk about your feelings of shame. Be truthful with someone you trust about what social norms you believe you violated so that you can understand where the feeling of shame is coming from and stop feeding it by holding it in. Remember, the more you try to repress your feelings, the stronger they become. Accept that you're experiencing shame, hear the thoughts, and either actively reframe them or do something to right the wrong. Try to link it to something specific you did, rather than who you are. Feeling shame doesn't mean you have some defect in your character.

A variety of situations can bring on shame, and in a sense, it can be a useful emotion that helps keep our behaviors in line. Sometimes, however, as with other emotions, people can really struggle under the weight of shame. Let's say you're rejected by a potential friend or new love interest and feelings of shame surface. Many people put themselves out there and find themselves rejected. It doesn't mean that there's something wrong with you compared with everyone else. It just indicates that it wasn't the right match. You can talk through your feelings with a friend to see it in a more realistic light.

One of the most painful parts of shame is that it can make you feel isolated and lonely. That's why it's crucial to bring shame to light, look at it, express it, and find ways to let it go. The more you challenge negative self-talk and treat yourself with compassion, the better you can combat feelings of shame.

TAKE A BANANA FOR A WALK

Dr. Albert Ellis developed a quirky exercise to combat shame. You walk a banana down the street as if you were walking a dog. It sounds silly, but there's a point to it. You will get many reactions from people who see you, but you just focus on the task at hand. The banana exercise can initially make you feel anxious and ashamed, but it has the potential to be freeing—and even a lot of fun.

Time: 10 minutes

Format: Behavioral activity

Instructions: Get a banana and a long cord. Tie the cord around the banana, put on your walking shoes, and go for a walk holding the cord and letting the banana "follow

you." Some passersby may laugh, others might be confused, some may not even notice, and others might ask you what you are doing. Well, you're just taking a banana for a walk.

You'll discover that nothing terrible will happen even if you're doing something that others might not approve of or understand. It's symbolic of how we feel judged and ashamed when we believe we've violated some social norm or when other people remark on our character or life choices. The reality is that people may judge your actions. However, you don't have to let it impact you.

Before you do this exercise, jot down some things you think might happen and how much shame you think you'll feel.

_____

_____

_____

After you've walked the banana, write about what actually happened and how much shame you actually felt.

_____

_____

_____

PRACTICE BEING VULNERABLE

One of the best ways to combat shame is to be vulnerable. If you picture a competition between shame and vulnerability, as you become more comfortable being vulnerable through being open and honest, you can decrease your sensitivity to feeling shame in the future. Vulnerability is a powerful tool that can help you overcome shame and get more comfortable with yourself.

Time: 10 minutes

Format: Conversation

Instructions: Create an opportunity to reveal something vulnerable about yourself to a new friend or date. When you reveal something about yourself that is personal to a new friend or romantic interest, it's also an opportunity to grow closer together. It doesn't have to be something major, especially at first. Just share something and then see how the other person reacts and whether they share something with you, too.

Here's an example: Let's say that you're a parent getting to know another parent while your kids are playing. You don't know this person very well, but you can naturally share during the conversation that you struggle from panic attacks. Not only does your admission demonstrate vulnerability, but it can also bring you and the other person closer together. Maybe the other parent has anxiety or struggles with mental health in some other way. Once you share your experience with panic attacks, they may feel more comfortable opening up about their own issues. Then, by receiving support and validation from one another, the two of you discover that there's nothing to be ashamed about.

WORK THROUGH A SHAMEFUL MEMORY

When you think back to your childhood, or maybe even recall a recent event, something may come to mind that causes you to feel shame. Don't try to make it go away. Instead, work through it to understand it better and learn from it.

Time: 10 minutes

Format: Written exercise

Instructions: Respond to the following prompts:

What is the shameful memory?

Jot down everything you remember about the situation. Where were you? What were you doing? What happened? Who was there? What did they say or do?

_____

_____

_____

_____

What triggered you to feel shame?

_____

_____

What was your physiological response; that is, what did you feel in your body when you felt shame?

_____

_____

What did you do in response to the shame?

_____

_____

Are your underlying beliefs about yourself accurate or helpful? How can you view the situation in a different way? Can you be a little more compassionate toward yourself? What would you say to a friend or loved one in a similar situation? What would this version of you say to that younger version?

_____

_____

_____

_____

_____

_____

_____

_____

_____

_____

_____

After analyzing the situation that caused you shame, you will better understand your triggers and consequences and then be able to start to work through the negative thoughts associated with that situation. Everyone has unique triggers, and it's crucial to work on yours. That way you can get to the source of your shame.

LESSONS LEARNED

Guilt and shame are heavy feelings. No one wants to feel them all the time, but, as you've learned, we need to feel them from time to time, as uncomfortable as they are, and if they are excessive or unreasonable, there are techniques we can use to work through them to feel better. Guilty feelings often arise when we overindulge, do something unkind or thoughtless, or are on the receiving end of a guilt trip (either from ourselves or someone else) for some perceived slight or wrongdoing. You have strategies to cope with all these scenarios. And if shame has you in its grip, you now know the importance of expressing it, looking at its source, challenging faulty beliefs, and being vulnerable. Flip back through this chapter and review your entries. Think about the experiences you had with each exercise. Respond to the following prompts:

Which exercise was most helpful and why?

_____

_____

Which exercise was your least favorite? Do you need to give it another try?

_____

_____

Did you skip any exercises? Why?

_____

_____

What is the most valuable lesson you learned from this chapter?

_____

_____

_____

_____

What do you still need to work on?

_____

_____

_____

_____

What is the next action you will take and when will you take it?

_____

_____

_____

_____

6

COPING WITH CONSTANT CRAVINGS

Cravings are natural urges, but they can become problematic or dangerous if you can't control them and instead overindulge in them. For many of us, coping with cravings is a constant struggle. Keep in mind that no matter how intense a craving is, it will pass. Whether it's for food, drugs, alcohol, or something else, all cravings rise in intensity, peak, and then fall. If you're having trouble coping with cravings and riding them out, this chapter is for you. The more you learn to tolerate cravings and not act on them, the more confident you will be in your ability to work through them in the future. It's okay to ask a trusted friend or family member for help while you develop the coping skills to manage your cravings. If an active addiction is the source of your craving, it's crucial to work with

a therapist in conjunction with the work you are doing in this workbook.

Cravings are often connected in some way with our basic needs. Perhaps not surprisingly, then, certain areas of the brain have been connected to what we experience when we fulfill a craving. Dopamine, a key hormone in the brain, is linked to feelings of pleasure, and we tend to crave things that cause an increase in dopamine because it makes us feel good. You can get a release of dopamine and the subsequent increase in pleasure from a number of sources—food, sex, risk-taking, certain substances, enjoyable activities, and so on. The greater the dopamine release, the more likely you'll want to engage in that activity again. So if you're not careful, you can quickly find yourself chasing a dopamine high by overdoing certain things.

Scientists believe that people who struggle with addictive behaviors (e.g., around food, sex, drugs, etc.) crave those things so their bodies can produce more dopamine. Similarly, the hormone oxytocin (the "love hormone") is also known to play a role in the reward centers of our brains. As such, there has been an increasing interest in oxytocin's role in addictions. Regardless of whether your cravings are run-of-the-mill or more serious, practicing your CBT skills can help you get a handle on them.

FOOD CRAVINGS

If you find that food is your go-to even when you're not hungry, you are not alone. Many people have very similar struggles. It's vital to learn to listen to your body and learn what factors influence your food cravings. Emotions such as stress can impact food cravings. Some people overeat when they're stressed, ignoring their hunger signals and continuing to eat even though they're satiated. Others undereat due to low appetite, anxiety, or slowed stomach motility caused by the stress reaction. The solution here is to focus on reducing your stress levels rather than getting caught up in the eating pattern. That way, you can get your body and mind to send accurate signals to each other, and your eating pattern should normalize.

Be cautious about diet fads, and be careful not to get caught up in dangerous "diet culture," which places a high value on weight, shape, and size while ignoring the health or emotional well-being of the person. The reality is that size isn't always a good predictor of health, but focusing exclusively on being a certain size is a good predictor of psychological problems. In other words, being rigid about what and how much you eat can lead to disordered eating and other psychological disorders such as depression and feelings of low self-esteem. Instead of chasing the latest diet fad, focus on creating your own customized wellness plan.

Many people who want to develop a healthy relationship with food practice intuitive eating. Intuitive eating philosophy suggests that when you get to the point of excessive hunger, your mind can't reason what to eat. That's why it's crucial to honor your body's signals and eat when you are hungry. In other words, if you want to eat, eat. Trust your instincts and intuition and consume food when you feel hunger. Just make sure you're aware of what you're eating and why. Pay attention to your cravings and think about where they are coming from. Be deliberate about what you eat and how much you eat. Here are some exercises that can help you on your journey to combat food cravings.

RATE YOUR HUNGER

You may not recognize your body's signs of hunger and satiety. There are physical signs that you're hungry or full. If you've ignored these signals for a long time, it can be challenging to recognize them. If you've engaged in restriction or bingeing, you might not

recall or have learned what it feels like to be appropriately hungry or full. That's where the hunger scale can help.

Time: 10 to 15 minutes

Format: Observation

Instructions: To increase your awareness of how it feels to be hungry and full and set the stage to learn mindful eating, do the following:

1. Before you sit down to eat a meal, rate how hungry you are on a scale from 0 to 10 (with 10 being the most hungry).

2. In the middle of your meal, rate your level of hunger again.

3. When you're finished with your meal, give your level of hunger a final rating.

The more you practice rating your hunger, the better you will learn to interpret the messages your body is sending you. That includes how much to eat when you're feeling hungry (based on how hungry you actually feel) and when to stop eating (when you actually feel full).

What did you learn from this experience?

_____

_____

CHILL BEFORE YOU EAT

Feelings of hunger might be triggered by emotions like stress, anxiety, or depression. It's important to nourish yourself so you can be energetic and productive. But being stressed, anxious, or depressed can work against you—both emotionally (you may end up feeling guilty) and physiologically (you may end up feeling tired, bloated, or unmotivated)—as you eat. Plus stress-related tension can make for an unpleasant eating experience. Before you start eating, take some time to calm your mind and body. The goal of this exercise is

to increase the quality of mealtime by being more mindful about what you eat, to reduce the chances of digestive problems, and to associate eating with pleasant feelings.

Time: 5 to 10 minutes

Format: Observation and written exercise

Instructions: Instead of immediately eating as soon as you have your food, try the following:

1. Notice how you are feeling and take notes:

2. Set a timer for five minutes. Sit in a chair, close your eyes, and take several slow, deep breaths. With every inhale, feel the tension in your muscles, and with every exhale, release the tightness. Start with the muscles in your head, face, and neck, and move from muscle to muscle down to your feet.

3. When the timer goes off, jot down how you feel. Identify any cognitive distortions that came up and reframe them here:

4. Focus on your meal and enjoy it, being mindful about how much to eat to satisfy your hunger.

TRY THE RAISIN MEDITATION

The raisin meditation is an excellent way to focus on slowing things down when you eat and to better understand your cravings. While you can choose any simple food that you

enjoy eating for this exercise, a popular choice for many people is a raisin. The task here is to eat a raisin mindfully.

Time: 5 to 10 minutes

Format: Mindfulness and written exercise

Instructions: Get a box of raisins, sit at a table, remove one raisin, and do the following activity:

1. Hold the raisin between your finger and thumb and focus on it.

2. Pretend you're seeing a raisin for the first time. Study the color and the wrinkled texture. Take in the raisin's scent. Examine its shadow. Roll the raisin between your fingertips. Close your eyes and listen to the sound of your fingers running over the raisin. You're now engaging all of your senses. You may be salivating at this point.

3. Put the raisin into your mouth, but do not bite down on it. Just feel it on your tongue. Bring focus to how it feels in your mouth as you move it around with your tongue. Then slowly and deliberately move it to your molars and take one bite. Notice what happens. Savor how it tastes.

4. Slowly chew on it and notice the flavor of it spread throughout your mouth. Where on your tongue do you experience the taste first? Where next? Experience the sounds and motions of chewing and everything else associated with eating it. When you're ready, swallow it.

5. After you finish eating the raisin, reflect on the experience. Respond to the following questions:

What did you learn from the raisin meditation?

What surprised you about mindfully eating a single raisin?

_____

_____

What sensations did you feel as you ate it?

_____

_____

What thoughts ran through your mind?

_____

_____

What did you learn from this experience with regard to your food cravings?

_____

_____

_____

EAT IN SILENCE

It's natural to want to have social meals. You go out to eat with your friends or have family dinners. You sit with your loved ones and talk about the events of the day. That's a great bonding experience, but there are other ways to enjoy your food and bring more

awareness to what and why you are eating, which can help you better understand your food cravings. Eating in silence is one of them.

Time: 5 to 10 minutes

Format: Mindfulness and written exercise

Instructions: Eat a meal in silence. Turn off the radio, phone, or television, and let anyone you are eating with know that you can have your scintillating conversations later.

As you eat, embrace the silence. Initially, you may feel strange not having the chatter of your company, but you may discover that the silence is refreshing and relaxing. When you focus entirely on the food, you are giving the act of eating all of your attention. If negative thoughts pop up, notice them, but then return your focus to the meal.

If you later crave food, you can remind yourself of this mindful experience and ask yourself if giving in to your craving will have the same effect.

Respond to the following prompts:

What did you think would happen during the silent meal?

_____

_____

_____

What actually happened? Describe your experience.

_____

TIP: If your family normally eats together at mealtimes, you can make this a fun game. The first person who talks has to clear away the dishes! If you live alone, an alternative to this would be to eat an entire meal in the dark (careful of hot foods, though!).

DON'T JUDGE YOUR CRAVINGS

Many of us struggle with intrusive thoughts around our eating patterns. There's a lot of pressure in society to eat the right thing, along with myriad opinions on what the "right thing" is. The food you're craving might be alerting you that you need a certain nutrient. Instead of judging your craving for salty chips, for instance, as bad or weak, think about whether your diet is too low in sodium. You know your body and what it needs and doesn't need. If you're concerned about your food choices, you can consult a dietitian.

Time: 10 to 15 minutes

Format: Mindfulness

Instructions: Take a moment to notice that you're having a craving for a particular food. You don't have to respond to the craving right away. It's important to not act impulsively. Wait five minutes.

If the craving persists, ask yourself, "If I respond to this craving, how will I feel afterward?" If you reply that you won't feel good but you still want it, avoid judging yourself. Not all food cravings are bad. Your body might need the nutrients. Consider if there's an alternative food that could help you satisfy your body and that *would* make you feel good if you ate it.

Whether or not you decide to eat the food you are craving, going through this process helps you make a mindful choice. If you do choose to eat what you're craving, give yourself the same nonjudgmental courtesy you would give a friend. Remind yourself that you're doing the best you can to manage your food cravings and care for your well-being.

DEALING WITH CRAVINGS IN GENERAL

We've focused a lot on food cravings so far, but people can crave all sorts of things. Whether you struggle with food or something else, there are a number of skills you can develop to combat your cravings. Mindfulness, which you just practiced, is one of them.

Mindfulness teaches us to stay in the moment, observing what's going on within and around us without any judgment. Mindfulness has been shown to help people manage their anxiety and enhance a person's awareness of their behavioral options. It also aids emotion regulation and improves overall wellness. Current and growing

research on mindfulness points to robust benefits that can positively impact nearly every aspect of our lives. You can practice mindfulness by sitting for just a few minutes a day and observing your thoughts, emotions, and sensations, or you can do a walking mindfulness exercise where you pay attention to your surroundings. In fact, you can do just about any activity mindfully. The important thing is to practice staying present without judgment. Once you start to feel comfortable with mindfulness, you can increase how often and how long you are mindful each time and then begin to apply it to more challenging situations (e.g., negative emotions and cravings).

Let's explore how mindfulness and other techniques can help you cope with your cravings.

S.T.O.P. FIRST

Instead of giving in to a craving, use the S.T.O.P. technique to identify the origin of the craving. S.T.O.P. stands for Stop, Take a deep breath, Observe, and Proceed. Psychologist Elisha Goldstein developed this technique using mindfulness-based practices to help return you to the present. When you take time to S.T.O.P., your thinking will be clearer, and you can make a choice based on that clarity.

Time: 5 to 10 minutes

Format: Mindfulness and written exercise

Instructions: The next time you find yourself craving something and want to give in to it, do the following:

1. Stop. Regardless of what you're doing, stop.

2. Take a deep breath. Breathing brings you into the present moment.

3. Observe. Look around you and see what's going on outside you. Feel what's going on inside of you. Note what you are thinking and feeling. Ask yourself, "What am I thinking? What is the craving urging me to do? What will happen if I act on this urge?"

4. Proceed. Continue with what you were doing.

Being mindful when a craving comes on can help decrease your tendency toward self-destructive behaviors. Respond to the following prompt:

When you tried the S.T.O.P. technique, what did you discover about your craving?

_____

_____

_____

Cravings can feel incredibly overwhelming when you're in the midst of them. One reason these urges are so intense is because of the attention you give them. Instead of acting on the craving, try to delay it, even for a short time. Once you see that it's possible to delay acting on a craving, you'll feel more confident that you can do it again. When another sudden urge comes in the future, you can remind yourself that you were able to ride out the urge in the past. This way, you're training your brain to tolerate intense urges. Waiting out cravings is an excellent way to learn to cope with them.

Time: 10 to 15 minutes

Format: Mindfulness and written exercise

Instructions: When you feel a craving coming on, do the following to delay acting on it:

1. Take a few intentional breaths.

2. Look around the room, choose five things you can see, and name them aloud.

3. As you look around the room, also observe the sensations in your body. Allow your muscles to relax.

4. Count to 10 while observing your body's sensations. With time, the craving will likely get less and less intense.

5. After 5 minutes, check in with yourself. If you notice that the urge is less intense or has passed, congratulate yourself. If not, repeat!

After you've done this activity, respond to the following prompts:

What were you craving?

_____

What did you notice about your body's response to delaying acting on the craving?

_____

_____

Did any cognitive distortions come to mind? If so, reframe them.

_____

_____

_____

Did the urge pass or become less intense? If no, why not? If yes, what helped?

_____

_____

_____

DISTRACT YOUR ATTENTION OR LEAVE THE SITUATION

An intense craving can seem like it has taken over your mind and body to the point where you feel out of control, especially when it comes on suddenly. There are things you can do to help yourself amid sudden impulses. If the urge is too strong to resist, it's okay to engage in a distraction or even leave the situation if you need to. In many instances, avoiding or escaping is not productive, but in this case, it is perfectly fine! You are protecting yourself.

Time: 15 to 20 minutes

Format: Behavioral activity and written exercise

Instructions: The next time you experience an intense craving, if possible, exit the physical space you're in to get away from the triggers and make it harder to access the thing you are craving. For example, maybe you're in the grocery store surrounded by food you want to take home and binge on, and you start to feel powerless not to grab it off the shelf.

First, remind yourself that you ultimately have control over your behavior. Then step outside and go for a walk. By leaving the situation, you are taking the power into your own hands. Plus, a change of scenery can reset your brain and help distract you from painful feelings.

If you can't remove yourself from the situation, you can do something else to distract yourself. Turn on the television, listen to music, play a game, call a friend, and so on. Distraction isn't always a bad thing. It's helpful to divert your attention when you're struggling. You're not weak for distracting yourself; rather, you're engaging in self-care.

List three to five distractions you can engage in when you're faced with an intense craving.

1. _____

2. _____

3. _____

4. _____

5. _____

DISENGAGE

Experiencing a craving is an uncomfortable sensation. It seems as if there's nothing you can do to satisfy the urge. The reality is that you can substitute something else for self-destructive behavior. The three As for managing triggers are: avoid the trigger, alter the trigger, or try an alternative.

Time: 15 to 20 minutes

Format: Behavioral activity and written exercise

Instructions: As soon as you notice a craving, substitute that urge for something that will promote long-term health. For example, if you have a problem controlling your urges to drink alcohol, step one is to avoid having easy access to it (i.e., get it out of your home). Next, if you have an urge to drink alcohol, instead try an alternative, such as a mocktail, sparkling water, a cup of tea, or something else that is healthy and makes you feel good. It's not the same thing as drinking alcohol, but you're giving yourself a healthy option that isn't a long-term detriment to your physical and mental health. Exercise is also a good choice, because it not only makes it hard to indulge a craving but also provides a natural high via a dopamine boost. (Make sure your doctor approves it before you start, though.)

It can help to have a list of healthy substitutes available for unhealthy cravings so you don't have to think for too long about what to substitute when an urge strikes. Use the following chart to come up with healthy alternatives to the things you crave. You can have several alternatives for one type of craving.

CRAVING	ALTERNATIVE

Now you have an arsenal of healthy alternative solutions you can draw upon when you're feeling sudden urges. Take a snapshot of this list and keep it with you, so no matter where you are when you're struggling, you have it available.

CALMING CRAVINGS FOR AN ADRENALINE RUSH

Sometimes people crave the adrenaline rush they get when they engage in a particular activity or consume a particular substance. The hormone adrenaline occurs in the body when you're excited or afraid. As soon as it enters the bloodstream, your heart races, your palms may sweat, and you may feel exhilarated. People who crave this feeling always seem to be chasing the next rush. Some may engage in thrilling activities such as extreme sports or pursue intense jobs like emergency medical technician, whereas others may choose self-destructive behaviors.

It's okay to seek out excitement, but there's a balance between having fun and hurting yourself. People who crave adrenaline rushes sometimes struggle with living in moderation and may open themselves up to problems such as substance abuse. In fact, research published in 2014 in *Substance Abuse and Rehabilitation* has shown that there are similarities in the brains between high-sensation-seeking athletes and substance abusers.

VISUALIZE A CALM PLACE

Guided imagery is a technique that can calm whatever is triggering you to chase the adrenaline high. The idea is to visualize yourself in a serene place, such as the ocean or a rain forest—wherever you feel calm. You can do this on your own or with the help of a narrator who guides you through the visualization. You can find guided visualization on YouTube or in audiobooks. In this exercise, the ocean will be the location, and you will be your own guide.

Time: 15 to 20 minutes

Format: Visualization

Instructions: Guide yourself through the visualization and then respond to the prompt:

1. Go someplace where you can be alone and set a timer.

2. Get comfortable and close your eyes.

3. Imagine yourself on a warm, sandy beach, lying on a comfortable blanket. Feel the sun's rays on your skin. Observe the sounds around you: Hear the waves crashing on the shore and the seagulls calling overhead. Smell and taste the salty air.

4. Relax in this space until the timer goes off.

Write down how the meditation made you feel and note any automatic thoughts you had.

_____

_____

_____

TRY LOW-INTENSITY EXERCISE

Adrenaline seekers are often looking for high-intensity exercises to trigger the rush. It may sound counterintuitive, but engaging in an opposite type of activity when you are experiencing a craving can help you get a handle on it. A low-intensity exercise will force your brain to calm down and train it to appreciate being grounded as a pleasurable experience.

Time: 30 to 60 minutes

Format: Physical activity and written exercise

Instructions: Choose a low-impact exercise you think you might enjoy to replace a thrill-seeking activity. Here are two options to consider:

→ **Yoga:** This is an excellent low-impact exercise. Adrenaline seekers put a lot of strain on their bodies. When you practice yoga, you're helping strengthen your mind and body. According to research published in the *International Journal of Yoga* in 2011, regular yoga practice can calm the adrenal system and promote adrenal health, which can help curb your craving for adrenaline-seeking activities. Overactive adrenal glands can be taxing on

your entire system. Yoga helps with learning new skills that facilitate the mind–body connection. When you're learning new yoga poses, it decreases activity in the hypothalamus, as found in a study published in *Ancient Science of Life*. The hypothalamus is the part of the brain that's responsible for how we express our feelings.

→ **Tai chi:** This noncompetitive martial art helps the practitioner get in tune with their body. There are many different movements to learn, and each movement flows into the next; your body is always moving, and it requires intense focus. Tai chi has a variety of styles. It helps people maintain their physical and mental health and gives them a chance to redirect their energy into a meditative and skill-based martial art.

List a few low-impact exercises or activities you might like to try the next time you find yourself craving a thrill and rate how likely you think each will be to help:

TAP INTO A SENSE MEMORY

This exercise, which actors sometimes use to get into character, can help you learn to calm your mind and body. It involves remembering physical sensations associated with a personal object. Sense memory uses emotional experiences to bring out particular feelings. There are times when an adrenaline rush can be triggered in you, and it can be hard to come down from that high, but with this exercise, you can begin to recall pleasant feelings and help get yourself back to a grounded state.

Time: 10 to 20 minutes

Format: Visualization and written exercise

Instructions: If you're so wound up that you can't imagine slowing down, take a deep breath and then do the following:

1. Bring to mind a joyful or calm recollection.

2. As you think of that pleasant memory, hold or imagine holding an object that's precious to you and is related to that memory. It could be something from childhood or a more recent time. For example, if you have fond memories of baking cookies with a loved one, you may choose to envision holding a ball of cookie dough in your hand and smelling the cookies baking.

3. Envision yourself handling or playing with the object. Notice if the memory conjures up warm feelings in you, which will likely be the case.

4. Do this for 10 to 15 minutes and then respond to the following prompts:

What object conjures up a feeling of joy or calmness?

_____

_____

_____

_____

Describe the memory associated with it.

_____

_____

_____

_____

How do you feel after doing this activity?

_____

_____

_____

_____

LESSONS LEARNED

Whatever you crave, you now have skills to practice that will help you to control that craving. The first step is to improve your awareness and mindfulness skills. These will help you see that you have choices when it comes to how you respond to a craving. Whether that means delaying your craving for just a few minutes or walking away from it entirely, the power is back in your hands. With cravings, distracting yourself from them can help, and so can replacing them with something you find enjoyable that's a healthy alternative. Flip back through this chapter and review your entries. Think about the experiences you had with each exercise. Respond to the following prompts:

Which exercise was most helpful and why?

_____

_____

Which exercise was your least favorite? Do you need to give it another try?

_____

_____

Did you skip any exercises? Why?

_____

_____

What is the most valuable lesson you learned from this chapter?

_____

_____

_____

_____

What do you still need to work on?

_____

_____

_____

_____

What is the next action you will take and when will you take it?

_____

_____

_____

_____

A Final Word

You've reached the end of the workbook! Take a moment to congratulate yourself and note this amazing accomplishment. We're so glad you've made it. It's our hope that you now have an introductory grasp of the tools described in these pages. In time, and with practice, using these tools will help you reframe your negative thoughts and in turn modify your feelings and broaden your behavioral repertoire. Remember that you can (and we advise you to) revisit these chapters from time to time for a refresher. CBT teaches lifelong tools that you can apply to any situation you're experiencing—but you need to keep the tools sharp and ready at your disposal.

We think you're holding an excellent, comprehensive cognitive behavioral therapy toolbox in your hand right now. But it will do you no good just sitting on your bookshelf or nightstand! You need to *practice*. And struggle. And make mistakes. And keep going. Hopefully, this workbook has given you more self-awareness as well as some confidence to practice CBT in your daily life. We wish you the best of luck in reframing your thoughts and bestow on to you the power to face challenging situations, correct cognitive distortions, and change problematic behaviors in the years ahead.

The 10 Cognitive Distortions

1. **All-or-nothing thinking**

2. **Overgeneralization**

3. **Mental filtering**

4. **Disqualifying the positive**

5. **Jumping to conclusions**

6. **Magnification or minimization**

7. **Emotional reasoning**

8. **"Should" statements**

9. **Labeling and mislabeling**

10. **Personalization**

Resources

WEBSITES

Beck Institute for Cognitive Behavior Therapy—Tools and Resources: BeckInstitute.org /tools-and-resources

National Alliance on Mental Illness: NAMI.org

Academy of Cognitive Behavioral Therapy: AcademyOfCT.org

Anxiety & Depression of Association of America (ADAA): ADAA.org

Association for Behavioral and Cognitive Therapies: ABCT.org

Centre for Clinical Interventions: CCI.health.wa.gov.au/Resources/Looking -After-Yourself

Dr. Simon Rego's website: SimonRego.com

RECOMMENDED READING

The ACT Workbook for Depression and Shame: Overcome Thoughts of Defectiveness and Increase Well-Being Using Acceptance and Commitment Therapy by Matthew McKay, Michael Jason Greenberg, and Patrick Fanning. Oakland, CA: New Harbinger Publications, 2020.

Anger Control Workbook: Simple, Innovative Techniques for Managing Anger and Developing Healthier Ways of Relating by Matthew McKay and Peter Rogers. Oakland, CA: New Harbinger Publications, 2000.

The Assertiveness Workbook: How to Express Your Ideas and Stand Up for Yourself at Work and in Relationships by Randy Paterson. Oakland, CA: New Harbinger Publications, 2000.

The Beck Diet Solution: Train Your Brain to Think Like a Thin Person by Judith S. Beck. Birmingham, AL: Oxmoor House, 2008.

Cognitive Behavioral Therapy Made Simple: 10 Strategies for Managing Anxiety, Depression, Anger, Panic, and Worry by Seth Gillihan. Emeryville, CA: Althea Press, 2018.

Cognitive Behavior Therapy: Basics and Beyond, 3rd Edition by Judith S. Beck. New York: The Guilford Press, 2011.

The Cognitive Behavioral Workbook for Weight Management: A Step-by-Step Program by Michele Laliberte, Randi E. McCabe, and Valerie Taylor. Oakland, CA: New Harbinger Publications, 2009.

End Emotional Eating: Using Dialectical Behavior Therapy Skills to Cope with Difficult Emotions and Develop a Healthy Relationship to Food by Jennifer Taitz. Oakland, CA: New Harbinger Publications, 2012.

Feeling Good: The New Mood Therapy by David D. Burns. New York: William Morrow and Company, 1980.

The Gratitude Project: How the Science of Thankfulness Can Rewire Our Brains for Resilience, Optimism, and the Greater Good by Jeremy Adam Smith, Kira Newman, Jason Marsh, and Dacher Keltner. Oakland, CA: New Harbinger Publications, 2020.

How to Accept Yourself: Overcoming Common Problems by Windy Dryden. London: Sheldon Press, 1999.

Mastery of Your Anxiety and Panic: Workbook by David H. Barlow and Michelle G. Craske. New York: Oxford University Press, 2007.

Mind Over Mood: Change How You Feel by Changing the Way You Think by Dennis Greenberger and Christine A. Padesky. New York: The Guilford Press, 2016.

Overcoming Depression One Step at a Time: The New Behavioral Activation Approach to Getting Your Life Back by Michael E. Addis and Christopher R. Martell. Oakland, CA: New Harbinger Publications, 2004.

The Relaxation and Stress Reduction Workbook by Martha Davis, Elizabeth Robbins Eshelman, and Matthew McKay. Oakland, CA: New Harbinger Publications, 2019.

The Seven Principles for Making Marriage Work: A Practical Guide from the Country's Foremost Relationship Expert by John M. Gottman and Nan Silver. New York: Harmony Books, 1999.

Ten Days to Self-Esteem by David D. Burns. New York: HarperCollins Publishers, 1993.

The 10-Step Depression Relief Workbook: A Cognitive Behavioral Therapy Approach by Simon Rego and Sarah Fader. Emeryville, CA: Althea Press, 2018.

References

The Albert Ellis Institute. "Rational Emotive Behavior Therapy." Accessed March 8, 2021. Albert Ellis.org/rebt-cbt-therapy.

Beck, Aaron T. *Cognitive Therapy and the Emotional Disorders*. New York: Penguin Group, 1979.

Beck Institute. "What Is Cognitive Behavior Therapy (CBT)?" Accessed March 8, 2021. BeckInstitute.org/get-informed/what-is-cognitive-therapy.

Burns, David D. *The Feeling Good Handbook: Using the New Mood Therapy in Everyday Life*. New York: William Morrow and Company, 1989.

Burns, David D. *Feeling Good: The New Mood Therapy*. New York: William Morrow and Company, 1980.

Chapman, Benjamin P., Kevin Fiscella, Ichiro Kawachi, Paul Duberstein, and Peter Muennig. "Emotion Suppression and Mortality Risk Over a 12-Year Follow-up." *Journal of Psychosomatic Research* 75, no. 4 (October 2013): 381–385. doi: 10.1016/j.jpsychores.2013.07.014.

Chapman, Gary. *The Five Love Languages: How to Express Heartfelt Commitment to Your Mate*. Chicago: Northfield Publishing, 1995.

Cherry, Kendra. "Psychologist Aaron Beck Biography: Founder of Cognitive Therapy." *Verywell Mind*. May 16, 2020. VerywellMind.com/aaron-beck-biography-2795492.

Cherry, Kendra. "What Is Cognitive Behavioral Therapy (CBT)?" *Verywell Mind*. Last modified June 13, 2020. VerywellMind.com/what-is-cognitive-behavior-therapy-2795747.

Cognitive Behavior Therapy Los Angeles. "Mindfulness STOP Skill." Accessed March 8, 2021. CogBTherapy.com/mindfulness-meditation-blog/mindfulness-stop-skill.

Congdon, Luis. "The One Thing Any Couple Can Do for Better Connection and Intimacy." *The Gottman Institute* (blog). March 7, 2017. Gottman.com/blog/the-one-thing-any-couple-can-do-for-better-connection-and-intimacy.

Cuijpers, Pim, Marit Sijbrandij, Sander L. Koole, Gerhard Andersson, Aartjan T. Beekman, and Charles F. Reynolds III. "Adding Psychotherapy to Antidepressant Medication in Depression and Anxiety Disorders: A Meta-analysis." *World Psychiatry* 13, no. 1 (2014): 56–67. doi: 10.1002/wps.20089.

DeRubeis, Robert J., Greg J. Siegle, and Steven D. Hollon. "Cognitive Therapy Versus Medication for Depression: Treatment Outcomes and Neural Mechanisms." *Nature Reviews Neuroscience* 9, no. 10 (September 2008): 788–796. doi: 10.1038/nrn2345.

Elisha Goldstein. "Mindfulness." *Mindfulness & Psychotherapy* (blog). Accessed March 8, 2021. ElishaGoldstein.com/mindfulness.

Harvard Health Publishing. "Understanding the Stress Response: Chronic Activation of This Survival Mechanism Impairs Health." Last modified July 6, 2020. Health.Harvard.edu /promotions/harvard-health-publications/stress-management-approaches-for-preventing-and-reducing-stress.

Hedman Erik, Cristina Botella, and Thomas Berger. "Internet-Based Cognitive Behavior Therapy for Social Anxiety Disorder." In: Nils Lindefors and Gerhard Andersson, eds. *Guided Internet-Based Treatments in Psychiatry*. Cham, Switzerland: Springer, 2016. doi: 10.1007 /978-3-319-06083-5_4.

Kaczkurkin, Antonia N., and Edna B. Foa. "Cognitive-Behavioral Therapy for Anxiety Disorders: An Update on the Empirical Evidence." *Dialogues in Clinical Neuroscience* 17, no. 3 (September 2015): 337–346. doi: 10.31887/DCNS.2015.17.3/akaczkurkin.

Krishnakumar, Divya, Michael R. Hamblin, and Shanmugamurthy Lakshmanan. "Meditation and Yoga Can Modulate Brain Mechanisms That Affect Behavior and Anxiety—A Modern Scientific Perspective." *Ancient Science of Life* 2, no. 1 (April 2015): 13–19. doi: 10.14259/as.v2i1.171.

Lisitsa, Ellie. "The Four Horsemen: Criticism, Contempt, Defensiveness, and Stonewalling." *The Gottman Institute* (blog). April 23, 2013. Gottman.com/blog/the-four-horsemen-recognizing -criticism-contempt-defensiveness-and-stonewalling.

Loerinc, Amanda G., Alicia E. Meuret, Michael P. Twohig, David Rosenfield, Ellen J. Bluett, and Michelle G. Craske. "Response Rates for CBT for Anxiety Disorders: Need for Standardized Criteria." *Clinical Psychology Review* 42 (December 2015): 72–82. doi: 10.1016/j.cpr .2015.08.004.

Medical University of Vienna. "Dopamine: Far More than Just the 'Happy Hormone.'" Science-Daily. August 31, 2016. ScienceDaily.com/releases/2016/08/160831085320.htm.

Michl, Louisa C., Katie A. McLaughlin, Kathrine Shepherd, and Susan Nolen-Hoeksema. "Rumination as a Mechanism Linking Stressful Life Events to Symptoms of Depression and Anxiety: Longitudinal Evidence in Early Adolescents and Adults." *Journal of Abnormal Psychology* 122, no. 2 (May 2013): 339–352. doi: 10.1037/a0031994.

Monell Chemical Senses Center. "Images of Desire: Brain Regions Activated by Food Craving Overlap with Areas Implicated in Drug Craving." ScienceDaily. November 11, 2004. ScienceDaily.com/releases/2004/11/041108025155.htm.

National Domestic Violence Hotline. Accessed March 8, 2021. TheHotline.org.

O'Neill, Shannon. "Shame Is in the Eye of the Beholder." The Albert Ellis Institute. January 2, 2015. AlbertEllis.org/shame-eye-beholder.

The Original Intuitive Eating Pros. "10 Principles of Intuitive Eating." Accessed March 8, 2021. IntuitiveEating.org/10-principles-of-intuitive-eating.

Pappas, Stephanie. "7 Ways Friendships Are Great for Your Health." LiveScience. January 8, 2016. LiveScience.com/53315-how-friendships-are-good-for-your-health.html.

Paterson, Randy. *The Assertiveness Workbook: How to Express Your Ideas and Stand Up for Yourself at Work and in Relationships.* Oakland, CA: New Harbinger Publications, 2000.

Raevuori, Anu, Danielle M. Dick, Anna Keski-Rahkonen, Lea Pulkkinen, Richard J. Rose, Aila Rissanen, Jaakko Kaprio, Richard J. Viken, and Karri Silventoinen. "Genetic and Environmental Factors Affecting Self-Esteem from Age 14 to 17: A Longitudinal Study of Finnish Twins." *Psychological Medicine* 37, no. 11 (November 2007): 1625–1633. doi: 10.1017/S0033291707000840.

Reardon, Claudia L., and Shane Creado. "Drug Abuse in Athletes." *Substance Abuse and Rehabilitation* 5 (2014): 95–105. doi: 10.2147/SAR.S53784.

Rettner, Rachael. "Want to Live Longer? Get Some Friends." LiveScience. July 27, 2010. LiveScience.com/6769-live-longer-friends.html.

Romero-Martínez, A., M. Lila, S. Vitoria-Estruch, and L. Moya-Albiol. "High Immunoglobulin A Levels Mediate the Association between High Anger Expression and Low Somatic Symptoms in Intimate Partner Violence Perpetrators." *Journal of Interpersonal Violence* 31, no. 4 (February 2016): 732–742. doi: 10.1177/0886260514556107.

Trauer, James M., Mary Y. Qian, Joseph S. Doyle, Shantha M. W. Rajaratnam, and David Cunnington. "Cognitive Behavioral Therapy for Chronic Insomnia: A Systematic Review and Meta-analysis." *Annals of Internal Medicine*, 163, no. 3 (August 2015): 191–204. doi: 10.7326/M14-2841.

University of Zurich. "Psychotherapy Normalizes the Brain in Social Phobia." ScienceDaily. February 6, 2017. ScienceDaily.com/releases/2017/02/170206084235.htm.

Wilson, Sarah J., David F. Abbott, Dean Lusher, Ellen C. Gentle, and Graeme D. Jackson. "Finding Your Voice: A Singing Lesson from Functional Imaging." *Human Brain Mapping* 32, no. 12 (December 2011): 2115–2130. doi: 10.1002/hbm.21173.

Woodyard, Catherine. "Exploring the Therapeutic Effects of Yoga and Its Ability to Increase Quality of Life." *International Journal of Yoga* 4, no. 2 (July 2011): 49–54. doi: 10.4103/0973-6131.85485.

Wu, Katherine. "Love, Actually: The Science behind Lust, Attraction, and Companionship." Harvard University: *Science in the News* (blog). February 14, 2017. SITN.hms.harvard.edu /flash/2017/love-actually-science-behind-lust-attraction-companionship.

Young, Ron. "Soft Skills: The Primary Predictor of Success in Academics, Career and Life." *PAIRIN* (blog). July 13, 2018. PAIRIN.com/soft-skills-primary-predictor-success-academics -career-life.

Index

A

ABC model, 122–123, 140
Abuse, 72
Acceptance. *See also* Self-acceptance
  of other perspectives, 65–66
  of others, 67–68
Active listening, 52, 97–98
Acts of service love language, 62
Addictions. *See* Cravings
Affirmations, 31, 128–129
Aggression, 105–106
All-or-nothing thinking, 7
Anger
  about, 104
  communicating, 105–110
  expressing, 111–115
  justifiable, 104–105
  managing, 5–6
Anxiety
  about, 88–89
  and fear of failure, 99–103
  managing, 2, 5–6, 14, 90–94
  social, 90, 94–97
  types of, 89–90
Assertiveness, 107–111
Assertiveness Workbook, The (Paterson), 106
Automatic thoughts, 3

B

Banana-walking exercise, 141–142
Beck, Aaron, 1
Behavioral activation, 4, 28–29, 41–42
Behavior patterns, 2–3
Beliefs
  challenging, 3
  changing, 3
  core, 95–96
Biological factors to low self-esteem, 22
Black-and-white thinking. *See* All-or-nothing thinking
Boundary-setting, 54–56, 128–129
Brain changes, 12
Breakups, 21–22
Breathing exercises
  for anger management, 110–111
  for stress management, 86–87
Bullying, 21, 105

C

Calmness, 90–91, 163–164
Catastrophizing, 5
CBT. *See* Cognitive behavioral therapy (CBT)
Chapman, Gary, 61
Checking-in behaviors, 76–78
Cognitive behavioral therapy (CBT)
  about, 2
  benefits of, 4–7
  best practices, 12–15
  how it works, 2–4
  origins of, 1
  as a skills-based approach, 12
Cognitive distortions, 3, 5, 7–9, 124–125, 172

Shame
  about, 119, 140
  expressing, 141–145
  letting go of, 6
"Should" statements, 9
Silence, eating in, 155–156
Singing, 91–92
Social anxiety disorder (SAD), 90, 94–97
Social networks, 56–60
Stonewalling, 70
S.T.O.P. technique, 157–158
Strengths, 139
Stress
  and food cravings, 151, 152–153
  managing, 5–6, 84–88
Substance abuse, 6
Success, 102–103
Support systems, lack of, 22

T

Tai chi, 165
Therapists, 2, 7
Thought records, 3, 9–11
Thoughts
  automatic, 3, 24–25
  intrusive, 4

  managing, 12
  negative, 5, 136–138
  reframing, 3–4, 7, 9–11
Trauma, 23, 104, 134
Triggers
  environmental, 21
  managing, 162
  self-loathing, 134
  shame, 145
  stress, 87–88

U

Uncertainty, 14, 76–78

V

Visualizing
  anger, 110–111
  calm, 90–91, 163–164
  success, 102–103
Vulnerability, 142

W

Words of affirmation love language, 62

Y

Yoga, 164–165

Acknowledgments

We would like to thank the incredible team at Callisto Media for their support and guidance during this project. Simon would like to thank Sarah for being the driving force behind this project and, in so doing, role-modeling how to overcome procrastination! Sarah would like to thank her brilliant coauthor Simon Rego for his invaluable insight into the world of cognitive behavioral therapy. We are grateful to the mental health advocacy community for their loyalty and bravery. Thank you to groundbreaking psychologists such as Drs. Aaron Beck and Albert Ellis for their hard work in paving the way for the widespread use of cognitive behavioral therapy. Lastly, thank you to our readers for making this book possible. We sincerely hope that by practicing these exercises, your mental health can thrive—and we sincerely believe you can do it!

About the Authors

Simon A. Rego, PsyD, is a licensed clinical psychologist with 25 years of experience in cognitive behavioral therapy (CBT) and other evidence-based psychological treatments. He is chief of psychology, director of psychology training, and director of the CBT training program at Montefiore Medical Center, the academic medical center and University Hospital for Albert Einstein College of Medicine in the Bronx, New York. He is also an associate professor of psychiatry and behavioral sciences at Albert Einstein College of Medicine, one of the nation's premier institutions for medical education, basic research, and clinical investigation.

Dr. Rego is board certified in cognitive behavioral psychology by the American Board of Professional Psychology, certified in cognitive behavior therapy by the Canadian Association of Cognitive and Behavioural Therapies, and certified as a cognitive therapy trainer/consultant by the Academy of Cognitive and Behavioral Therapies. He is a fellow of the American Academy of Cognitive and Behavioral Psychology, the Association for Behavioral and Cognitive Therapies, and the Academy of Cognitive Therapy, as well as a founding clinical fellow of the Anxiety & Depression Association of America. He is listed in *Who's Who in America* and *Who's Who in Medicine Academia* and was the recipient of the 2008 award for Distinguished Early Career Psychologists by the New York State Psychological Association, the 2015 Peterson Prize from the Graduate School of Applied and Professional Psychology at Rutgers University, and the 2018 Jerilyn Ross Clinician Advocate Award from the Anxiety and Depression Association of America.

Sarah Fader is the cofounder of Stigma Fighters, a nonprofit organization that encourages people with mental illness to share their personal stories. She has been featured in *The New York Times, The Washington Post, The Atlantic, Quartz, Psychology Today, HuffPost, HuffPost Live,* and *Good Day New York.*